# The Macroeconomics of Transition

Debates about the transition of planned (Soviet-type) economies are becoming more intense. How successful has this transition been? For example, is the steep fall in output disastrous or an inevitable step on the path to a more efficient economic system? Are countries moving from a planned to a market economy too slowly or too quickly? The economics of transition has become a 'new frontier' for economists.

This book, edited by two Polish economists, Jan Winiecki and Andrzej Kondratowicz, offers a systematic account of macroeconomic and institutional developments in those East Central European countries which are most advanced in the transition process.

Four country reports, on Czecho-Slovakia, Hungary, Poland, and (former) Yugoslavia, deal with output, macro policies, wages, prices and employment, as well as with foreign trade and current account issues. They are preceded by a regional report stressing similarities and dissimilarities in the pattern of transition to the market and followed by an analysis of theorists' and policy makers' expectations regarding various aspects of transition. In this way *The Macroeconomics of Transition* assesses the accuracy and usefulness of economic theories in explaining and predicting this unprecedented transition process.

**Jan Winiecki** is Professor of Economics at the Catholic University of Lublin. He is currently on long-term leave, working at the European Bank for Reconstruction and Development. He is also President of the Adam Smith Research Centre in Warsaw. He has written extensively on the subject of Soviet-type economies and, more recently, their transition to the market.

**Andrzej Kondratowicz** is a lecturer in the Department of Economics, Warsaw University. He has studied both in Poland and the United States. He is also an associate of the Adam Smith Research Centre. His studies have focused on monetary economics and international trade and finance.

# The Macroeconomics of Transition

Developments in East Central Europe

Edited by
Jan Winiecki and Andrzej Kondratowicz

A book prepared in collaboration with the Adam Smith Research Centre, Warsaw

London and New York

First published 1993 by
Routledge
11 New Fetter Lane, London EC4P 4EE

Simultaneously published in the USA and Canada
by Routledge
a division of Routledge, Chapman and Hall, Inc.
29 West 35th Street, New York, NY 10001

© 1993 Jan Winiecki and Andrzej Kondratowicz

Typeset in Times by
Ponting–Green Publishing Services, Chesham, Bucks
Printed and bound in Great Britain by
Biddles Ltd, Guildford and Kings Lynn

*British Library Cataloguing in Publication Data*
A catalogue reference for this book is available from the
British Library.

ISBN 0–415–09167–5


*Library of Congress Cataloging-in-Publication Data*

The Macroeconomics of transition : developments in East
Central Europe / edited by Jan Winiecki and Andrzej
Kondratowicz.
    p.    cm.
Simultaneously published in the USA and Canada.
Includes bibliographical references and index.
ISBN  0–415–09167–5
1. Europe, Eastern–Economic conditions–1989–
2. Europe, Eastern–Economic policy–1989–   3. Mixed
economy–Europe, Eastern.
I. Winiecki, Jan.  II. Kondratowicz, Andrzej, 1953–.
HC244.M226   1993
330.947'0009'049–dc20             92–32041
                                  CIP

# Contents

# Figures and tables

# Preface

*Andrzej Kondratowicz and Jan Winiecki*

The project upon which this book is based took shape between late 1989 and early 1991. The events of that period, sometimes called the East European 'Spring of Nations' (even if happening in autumn), put Hungary, followed by Poland and then Czecho-Slovakia in the lead of the countries of the region undergoing the transition to democracy and a market economy. It seemed eminently sensible to put macroeconomic developments in those countries into a comparative perspective. Especially since these countries began their stabilization-cum-liberalization efforts at about the same time (give or take about a year).

Initial discussions resulted in extending the list of countries which were to be included in the emerging Ford Foundation-financed project. Although the democratic credentials of freshly converted Yugoslav communists seemed already somewhat doubtful at that time, the stabilization programme put into operation in Yugoslavia by the then Federal Government, under the aegis of the IMF, positively merited analytical interest.

Apart from that, it was thought worthwhile to look at the parallel hyperinflationary developments in Poland and Yugoslavia and at their outcomes, produced under basically similar 'heterodox' stabilization programmes. Given the geographical location of the countries concerned and all the existing historical connotations, the term 'East Central Europe' has been accepted for the project's title.

The Adam Smith Research Centre, a free-market oriented think-tank in Warsaw, has been able to line up analysts from four countries and the project, once approved,[1] started in spring 1991. The agreed format of the project was as follows: four country surveys, written by analysts from the respective countries, were preceded by an overall regional survey putting economy-specific developments into a comparative perspective. The latter was followed by a statistical appendix.

It was suggested to the authors that their surveys follow a stan-dard(ized) pattern of macroeconomic analysis, but with one possible exception or departure. Since macroeconomic developments were taking place within the unique framework of the transition from a planned Soviet-type economy to a capitalist market economy, the institutional factors were playing a much larger role than in the case of mature market economies. Therefore, an institutional section was included in each country survey. In addition, throughout each survey, the spotlight was put on the influence that those particular institutional factors had had on economic results.

In this way a unique product has emerged as a result of the project. On the one hand, it attempts to answer 'usual' macroeconomic ques-tions related to stabilization and liberalization. On the other hand, it links the latter to the institutional heritage of the past and the institutional change of the present day. The project co-ordinator – Adam Smith Research Centre (ASRC) – as well as all contributing authors and editors of this book express their hope that it shall improve the understanding of macroeconomic developments in East Central Europe.

In some respects the book differs from the final report submitted to the Ford Foundation. Those differences have partly been forced upon us by political developments in what used to be Yugoslavia. As a result of the civil strife there and the subsequent disintegration of the federal state, the final report dealt with the Croatian economy only. There were at least two good reasons for that. First, our country analyst from the former Yugoslavia happened to be a Croat. Second, under the new circumstances availability of data from other post-Yugoslav states declined dramatically, making the task of covering other than Croatian states almost impossible.

However, since the main idea of the project – and for that matter of the book – has been to present macroeconomic developments under the stabilization and liberalization programmes, the survey of war-torn Croatia did not fit the general theme of transition. Therefore, we have decided to use in the book our collaborator's report on Yugoslavia which was prepared earlier for the interim project report to Ford Foundation. This report dealt to a greater extent with the standard stabilization and liberalization issues. The only problem was that it covered the period until mid-1991 only. However, since stabilization-cum-liberalization developments have since then been overwhelmed by those which resulted from the civil strife, the main theme of the book has been, in our view, much better served by just presenting this earlier report.

If the foregoing should be considered as imposed upon us by external circumstances, then quite another difference has been the result of a fully intended decision of the editors. The final report – and consequently this book – has included a regional survey assessing the developments from a comparative perspective. But yet another approach merited interest: namely, confronting the expectations as to the transition's outcome with the real-life developments, as they actually occurred.

After all, transition started in some countries as early as the second half of 1989, and since then a lot of expectations may have been either confirmed or rejected. Thus, since one of the editors wrote in early 1992 a paper dealing with economic developments that were both expected and unexpected by – and even surprising to – theorists and policy makers, it has been decided to include this paper in the present book. (The paper was in the meantime published in a slightly condensed form in the *Banca Nazionale del Lavoro Quarterly Review* of June 1992.)

The editors hope that this extension of the original report will better serve the needs and interests of readers. For it will allow them to look at the fast-moving transition of post-Soviet-type economies in East Central Europe from yet another angle.

## NOTE

1 Ford Foundation Prime Grant #915–0397 to Pittsburgh University with the subcontract to ASRC as the final co-ordinator of the project (Subcontract #8934.1).

# 1  Regional survey

*Jan Winiecki*

## FORCES SHAPING ECONOMIC ACTIVITY

The countries of East Central Europe underwent far-reaching changes in 1991 (the period covered by the Ford Foundation-financed project). For most countries this was not the first year of the transition to the market economy (Czecho-Slovakia being an exception). Among forces shaping economic activity, a major role has been played by the transition programmes themselves, although other economic and political developments, internal and external, contributed significantly to macroeconomic outcomes.

As signalled, transition to the market system has been at different stages of progress in each of the countries in question. In Czecho-Slovakia the programme started only on 1 January 1991, but after a full year of preparation and macroeconomic restraint.

In Hungary, a persistent reformer under the communist regime, transition began earlier than elsewhere, in 1989. But after the 1990 parliamentary elections and the defeat of communists, the programme was cautiously reshaped by the new coalition government. The year 1991 witnessed a continuation of that cautious approach, with gradual reduction of subsidies, some tightening of monetary policy, and continuing liberalization of foreign trade and foreign exchange.

In Poland and in Yugoslavia the situation had been similar at the start but strikingly different at the year-end, largely for political reasons. At the start in both countries extreme disequilibria resulted in 1989 in hyperinflation and in both transition programmes began on 1 January 1990, coupled with macroeconomic restraint to squeeze out inflationary pressures. Over time, however, differences emerged, first economic and later political.

Thus, Polish monetary policy became too restrictive in the autumn of 1990, while Yugoslav monetary policy became traditionally lax, when serious strains began to be felt throughout the economy. The political and military developments of 1991 and the break-up of Yugoslavia put an end to the transition programme (that was in any case undermined by the unilateral decisions of various constituent republics).

In all countries concerned, macroeconomic policies basically continued to be aimed at reducing disequilibria and containing inflationary pressures, both those inherited from the past and those arising from price and foreign trade liberalizations. As the year progressed it became increasingly clear for some analysts that standard (so-called 'heterodox') stabilization programmes became, in the post-STE institutional environment, as much a part of the problem as a solution.

The programme in question, having been tried in some developing countries, is also seen as a useful tool in combating disequilibria in Eastern Europe. The present writer, however, takes exception to its unmodified applicability in the post-STE environment. Being too simplistic, it directly – and adversely – affects the transition through the operation of monetary policy under the drastically different ownership structure. Furthermore, the programme in question has serious – and again adverse – indirect consequences in the fiscal sphere, also due to the institutional inheritance from the STE regime. The serious difficulties that these consequences generate for employment in, and incomes of, state industrial and 'traditional' budget-financed sectors spill over to the political area, sharply reducing public support for the transition.

Monetary policy under the circumstances of 'nobody's' banks and 'nobody's' enterprises is not the only area singled out for criticism with regard to the standardized stabilization programme, as this author noted elsewhere.[1] The basic idea of 'heterodox' programmes is that not only actual inflation but also inflationary expectations should be addressed by macroeconomic and other policy measures. But the policy of so-called nominal 'anchors' adversely affects gains from trade resulting from external liberalization in the case of a fixed ('pegged') exchange rate and structural adjustment in the case of wage controls. All these issues are considered in the subsequent sections of this survey.

Obviously, the standard stabilization treatment is in need of a greater sophistication, taking into account institutional differences of post-STEs in transition *vis-à-vis* earlier practitioners of standardized stabilization programmes. There has been an urgent need to modify existing instruments or devise new ones that could be applied in parallel with the standard measures in order to tackle institution-specific problems of post-STEs. What should also be noted at this point, however, is yet another reason for macroeconomic restraint at the beginning of the transition from a persistently disequilibrated shortage economy to the market: it is the need for credibility of transition programmes and governmental policies.

The restrictive macroeconomic policy is expected not only to wring out inflationary pressures, both inherited from the past and reinforced by price liberalization, but also to change drastically the supply/ demand relationship. After a few decades of persistent excess demand, fall in demand caused by macroeconomic restraint is expected first of all to discipline economic agents, accustomed to 'soft' budget constraint.[2] For the first time in decades they are forced to search for buyers (rather than the other way round). This sobering experience increases the credibility of the transition programme in the short run, as state-owned enterprises (SOEs for short) are led to believe that the change is real.

Of course, economic agents may hope that, as restraint begins to bite, pressures will force the government to revert to the old ways: easy money, unlimited subsidies, etc. And this is what has been demanded from various quarters, most vocally in Poland, especially in the second half of 1991 and what had already happened to some extent in former Yugoslavia as early as autumn 1990.

Macroeconomic restraint at the start of a transition programme is a necessary condition of the programme's credibility, but it is not a sufficient one. Credibility is being constantly reinforced throughout the programme's implementation. Conversely, internal contradictions of the programme itself, policy concessions to populist demands and *ad hoc* subsidization of the state sector tend to erode credibility. From this viewpoint, 1991 witnessed the strongly increased credibility of the Czecho-Slovak programme, some enhancement of credibility of the Hungarian one, and its decrease in Poland and – largely for political reasons – a collapse of the Yugoslav programme.

Finally, macroeconomic developments in 1991 were affected by strongly adverse external economic conditions for the transition in East Central Europe. The most important has been the shift in trade with the former Soviet Union from the inconvertible transferable rouble to convertible currencies and the collapse of the economy there. The shift to dollar trade, conceived by Soviet decision-makers as a means of improving the Soviet balance of payments, also adversely affected the Soviet industrial output.

However, the immediate effect of the shift was the deterioration of trade balance of all smaller ex-COMECON countries. The collapse of the Soviet economy, accelerated after the failed communist coup in August 1991, added to the problems of countries in transition. Demand from that direction fell sharply, acute payment difficulties for deliveries to Soviet partners have been experienced, and there have been recurrent failures of the post-USSR parties to various supply agreements to actually deliver agreed quantities (in spite of the shift to payments in convertible currencies).

The disappearance of what used to be the German Democratic Republic in 1990 was another blow. Given the weak competitiveness of post-STEs, the ability to export to the world market the generally obsolete goods sold to these two countries, was rather limited. Since these two countries made up in 1988–9 about one third of total exports of East Central European economies in transition, the fall in demand from that direction in 1989–91 is comparable with, say, the disappearance of the United States' market for East Asian 'little dragons'.

Even without any further adverse developments, the foregoing in itself ensured that 1991 would be an extremely difficult year in terms of output. But this was not the end of adverse changes in the external environment. Iraqi aggression against Kuwait resulted in the suspension of trade, first with both Iraq and Kuwait and later with Iraq, while increased oil prices made another dent in the trade balance, although fortunately Iraq's defeat calmed the international oil market, and prices fell considerably in winter 1991. Finally, economic slowdown in the West reduced demand in the most important export market.

## OUTPUT PATTERNS UNDER MACROECONOMIC RESTRAINT

A combination of macroeconomic restraint associated with the stabilization and liberalization of economies in transition, coupled with the sharp fall in external demand, was sufficient to ensure a steep decline in output. Table 1.1 shows this clearly enough with respect to GDP (preliminary) and industrial output.

Gross Domestic Product declined in all countries under consideration, with the data for Croatia (that were substituted for those of Yugoslavia in a country survey) excluded from comparative tables due

*Table 1.1* Gross domestic product and industrial output: annual rate of change in per cent

|  | 1988 | 1989 | 1990 | 1991 |
|---|---|---|---|---|
| Gross domestic product |  |  |  |  |
| Czecho-Slovakia | 2.6 | 1.3 | −0.4 | −16.4 |
| Hungary | −0.1 | −0.2 | −4.0 | −(7–9) |
| Poland | 4.1 | 0.2 | −11.6 | −8.0 |
| Yugoslavia[a] | −1.7 | 0.8 | −7.5 | x |
| Industrial output |  |  |  |  |
| Czecho-Slovakia | 2.1 | 0.8 | −3.7 | −23.1 |
| Hungary | 0.0 | −3.4 | −9.2 | −13.0 |
| Poland | 5.3 | −0.5 | −24.2 | −11.9 |
| Yugoslavia | −0.7 | 0.9 | −10.3 | x |

*Note*: [a] Gross Social Product, i.e. about 7 per cent smaller than GDP

to obvious lack of comparability. The fall has been the largest, as expected by this analyst, in Czecho-Slovakia, since it was the first year of the stabilization programme in that country.

At the time of writing, i.e. mid-February 1992, the range of estimates is the decline within 12–17 per cent limits, with industrial output falling even further. This is understandable. Czecho-Slovak figures reflect not only the effects of initial macroeconomic squeeze at the start of the transition and those of the adverse external economic environment in 1991, but also the effects of the downward output adjustment associated with the shift away from the wasteful Soviet economic system (see below).

However, it should be noted that the figures are certainly overstated, as statistics in 1991 covered only enterprises employing 100 and more persons. This effectively excluded the fledgling private sector, which contributed about 1.2 per cent to industrial output, 5–6 per cent to construction output and 13 per cent to retail trade turnover. It excluded small SOEs as well.

GDP declined by 8–10 per cent in Poland and by 7–9 per cent in Hungary, again with industrial output declining by more. Surprisingly, in contrast to GDP, industrial output declined by more in Hungary than in Poland. Estimates for Hungary were at the time of writing about 13–15 per cent and for Poland 11.9 per cent respectively. More worrying than the decline *per se* has been the tendency for output to decline by more in the second than in the first half of 1991 in all three countries (also in former Yugoslavia, albeit for different, i.e. political, reasons). The rate of decline slowed down in the fourth quarter, though, which suggested the bottoming out of deep recession associated with the adjustment to the market system. The recession may be carried over into 1992, though. Prospects differ across countries, with most optimistic forecasts concerning Hungary, but, contrary to most expectations Poland is another candidate for positive, albeit small growth this year.

One should be wary, however, of making cross-country comparisons on the basis of the depth of output fall in order to evaluate, for example, the relative ability of each economy to adjust. Post-Soviet-type economies differ among themselves with respect to both the time that has passed since the beginning of the transition programme and the choice of a speed at which transition is being implemented. Also, the starting point of transition – much worse in Poland and Yugoslavia – affected the pattern of output. Furthermore, autonomous policy errors might have influenced the depth of output fall. This is what the present writer stressed with respect to Poland in the mid-1990 to mid-1991 period.[3]

One more issue, already signalled, is worth stressing here. The very shift from the wasteful Soviet economic system to the market system entails an autonomous fall in output. It is inevitable, as this analyst pointed out insistently,[4] that output not demanded under normal conditions would disappear on the way to the market.

The 'mystery of vanishing output' is, in fact, rather simple. The Soviet-type economy is known for its persistent shortages, to which economic agents, especially state enterprises (with 'soft' budget constraint), adapt by hoarding inputs, fixed assets and labour. Probably the best-known manifestations of that phenomenon are very high input inventory-to-output ratios in Soviet-type economies: between 60 and 100 per cent (in the mid-1980s it was over 80 per cent in the USSR and about 30 per cent in the United States).

Quite obviously, once macroeconomic restraint at the beginning of transition brings about the reversal of the traditional supply/demand relationship, state enterprises adjust to new conditions of excess supply by reducing their inventories and simultaneously lowering or altogether cancelling new orders for inputs, as well as by reducing orders for new machinery and equipment. Therefrom stems a fall in domestic demand for and output of raw materials, intermediate products, lathes and other machinery, transport equipment, etc.

This process has already been visible in Hungary since late 1988. In

Poland input inventories, after large increases during the hyperinfla-tionary phase in 1989, fell in industry by 17.8 per cent in real terms in 1990, and the process continued in 1991 (preliminary estimates show decline by a further 5 per cent). Somewhat puzzling in this context has been the behaviour of Czecho-Slovak enterprises that increased their input inventories in the first quarter of 1991 by 18.1 per cent but this seems to be an exception (for possible explanation, see the following section). In any case this development appears to have been reversed afterwards, to some extent.

Households, too, adjust to the re-emergence of goods in the shops by buying smaller quantities of, for example, food products. Earlier, they bought larger quantities whenever they could get hold of them, not knowing when they would be able to buy the next batch. Part of that food was spoiled before use.

The foregoing points to a very important conclusion with regard to the autonomous output fall in the transition period. Contrary to the usual evaluation of the decline in output, this should be treated not as a cost of transition but only as a phenomenon concomitant of the shift away from a wasteful economic system.

No less importantly, output fall stemming therefrom hardly reduces the aggregate level of economic welfare of a country undergoing transition. It simply signifies the fall in the use of inputs and other production factors per unit of enterprise output and the fall in purchases per unit of household consumption.

However, the benefits of higher efficiency are spread across the whole population, while the price of higher efficiency is paid by those made redundant as a result of reduced demand. But this makes the one-off downward output adjustment a phenomenon that should be dealt with through social, not economic policy measures.

## MONETARY AND FISCAL POLICIES

This brings us to the next issue to be considered, that is the monetary and fiscal stance in 1991 in the countries under consideration. It can be generally characterized as monetary restriction of various degrees of severity related to the stage of the transition process, the choice of a more rapid or gradual speed of transition and, finally, the decisiveness in pursuing stated goals. On the fiscal side, 1991 witnessed largely failed efforts at maintaining recently achieved budgetary balance. Fiscal crisis has been most strongly in evidence in Poland and, to a much smaller extent, also in Hungary in 1991, while the same is expected to happen in Czecho-Slovakia this year. This latter country started transition only on 1 January 1991, and therefore has not yet experienced the full effects of the fall in revenues from state-owned enterprises.

*Table 1.2*    Growth of money stock, credit expansion for the enterprise sector and level of interest rates[a] (in billion of units of national currency)

|  | 1988 | 1989 | 1990 | 1991 |
|---|---|---|---|---|
| *Czecho-Slovakia* | | | | |
| Money stock (M2) | 529.4 | 547.8 | 550.7 | 672.2 |
| Credit expansion | 543.8 | 530.8 | 536.0 | 640.5 |
| Interest rate | 5.1 | 5.7 | 6.0 | 10.0[b] |
| Memorandum item | | | | |
| Inflation rate (CPI) | 0.2 | 1.4 | 10.0 | 57.9 |
| *Hungary* | | | | |
| Money stock (M2) | 612.4 | 706.3 | 912.9 | 1010.5[c] |
| Credit expansion | 681.0 | 817.0 | 984.0 | 1018.0[c] |
| Interest rate | 13.0 | 17.0 | 28.0 | 29.0[d] |
| Memorandum item | | | | |
| Inflation rate (CPI) | 15.5 | 18.8 | 28.9 | 35.2 |
| *Poland* | | | | |
| Money stock | 11.3 | 26.3 | 129.0 | 204.7 |
| Credit expansion | 10.0 | 28.7 | 114.1 | 184.6 |
| Interest rate | 6.0 | 61.3 | 103.8 | 53.9 |
| Memorandum item | | | | |
| Inflation rate (CPI) | 59.0 | 259.5 | 584.7 | 70.3 |
| December–December | . | . | 249.5 | 60.3 |
| *Yugoslavia* | | | | |
| Money stock | 4.2 | 93.3 | 342.4 | 509.3[e] |
| Credit expansion | 3.9 | 88.4 | 163.5 | . |
| Interest rate | 253.5 | 324.5 | 203.0 | . |
| Memorandum item | | | | |
| Inflation rate (CPI) | 194.1 | 125.0 | 588.0 | x |
| December–December | . | . | 120.2 | x |

*Notes*: [a]central bank's main lending rate
[b]reduced to 9.5 per cent in the second half of 1991
[c]January–September 1991
[d]January–October 1991
[e]January–June 1991

The data in table 1.2 on the growth of money stock, credit expansion and the level of interest rates in four countries in question show basic monetary developments there. Even more than in the case of output, the data are not directly comparable, given the widely differing inflation patterns. An added memorandum item (Consumer Price Index) enables the reader to evaluate these developments roughly in real terms.

Thus, the most severe credit squeeze in 1991 took place in Czecho-Slovakia, where credits for state enterprises fell by 22.7 per cent in real terms. This is not surprising, as Czecho-Slovakia had begun its pro-gramme only that year, while the other countries under consideration started earlier, with the resultant changes in monetary policy. However, the severity of the credit squeeze is remarkable – comparable only to Polish restraint in the first half of 1990. In fact Czecho-Slovak monetary restraint may be even stronger, as in Poland it was the household sector, not an enterprise sector, that bore the brunt of restraint.

What is surprising, however, is that it is a relatively low level of interest rates that turned out to be such a deterrent: the central bank's main lending rate was 10 per cent (reduced slightly in the second half of 1991 to 9.5 per cent) and the commercial banks' rates for enterprises was 14–24 per cent on the average, both on an annual basis. In comparison with 57.9 per cent CPI increase in 1991, interest rates have been strongly negative in real terms.

It is probably for this very reason that many Czecho-Slovak enter-prises increased rather than decreased input inventories after the beginning of the transition – in contrast to their counterparts in other post-Soviet-type economies. Quick calculation showed that it would be profitable to use inputs subsidized in that way in higher priced products manufactured in the months to come. But if the foregoing was so unambiguous, why would there be such a dramatic fall in the volume of credit for state enterprises? There are two plausible answers on the demand side. One is that the lack of a severe inflationary past in Czecho-Slovakia made state enterprises generally much more cautious in this respect, and the 14–24 per cent annual interest rate seems to have been a strong enough deterrent to many of them, regardless of the level of present inflation – and of the incentive to increase inventories. Another is that informal credit ceilings for commercial banks were successfully applied.

Yet another interpretation looks at the supply side. Czecho-Slovak banks were reluctant to lend, since they had a very bloated portfolio of loans to SOEs inherited from the past. Therefore, old ties and lending inertia notwithstanding, they lent less than they could, even under credit rationing. In the view of the present writer, each of the interpretations is probably right and each might have influenced credit developments in 1991.

Analysts in all countries concerned note the emerging or increasing problems with state enterprises' response to new conditions of macro-economic restraint. The most obvious is the 'wait and see' attitude, i.e. the postponement of the adjustment in the hope that the government will reverse the policy direction, when output-cum-unemployment fall will have made their mark. The more often such policy reversals have happened in the recent past, the more entrenched such an attitude becomes. It was – until the outbreak of the civil war – most visible in Yugoslavia but not infrequent elsewhere.

Other responses were at work as well. The most noticeable has been a tendency on the part of enterprises to slow down payments to their suppliers and in this manner to force them to extend involuntary credit. As monetary restraint has been more or less continuing and subsidies were being reduced, this way of surviving without positive adjustment (i.e. without searching for new markets, new distribution channels, new products, etc.), spread ever wider.

In Czecho-Slovakia the phenomenon had been of insignificant size as late as at the end of 1989 but increased with the tight macroeconomic policy pursued in 1990 to 44.9 billion kcs in December and later grew at a very fast rate. It amounted to 78.6 billion kcs in March, 123.4 billion kcs in June, 147.1 in September and to 155 billion in December 1991.[5] Two assessments are worth noting. First, the last sum was equal to almost 25 per cent of the total credit volume in 1991. Second, there has been a tendency for the involuntary credit's growth rate to slow down.

In Hungary and Poland state enterprises have been playing the non-payment game for much longer. Accordingly, the volumes of inter-enterprise credit have been higher than in Czecho-Slovakia. In Hungary it increased steadily in recent years reaching 31.5 per cent of total credit volume for SOEs in December 1990 and 44.3 per cent in September 1991. In Poland it more than doubled from 47 to 103 trillion zl. between December 1989 and December 1990, and increased still further – although at a slower pace – to 170 trillion zl. in September 1991. The last two sums were about equal to all credits extended by banks to state enterprises. It has been yet another indication that Polish state enterprises seem to have been most active in avoiding positive adjustment.

Yugoslavia could in 1990 be placed somewhere between Hungary and Poland as far as this particular phenomenon is concerned. It may be assumed that the strife only increased the proclivity of firms to survive in the face of both political and economic pressures.

A question may be asked why creditor enterprises do not start bankruptcy proceedings against the debtors to recover their debt. First, state enterprises are not accustomed to do so; the still prevalent way of thinking is that it is the business of the state, not their own. Second, they do not want to ruin one of the few clients they have. Since positive adjustment (search for new clients) is rather slow, the already existing links are all the more valuable.

The involuntary credit poses obviously serious problems for macro-economic stabilization because it undermines the efficiency of monetary policy. It is no less harmful for microeconomic adjustment. Better enterprises, exposed to unexpected cash flow problems, have to rely on very costly short term credit as a result, which makes their financial situation more precarious as well. Remedial measures are slow in coming, though, even if the malady is well recognized.

The foregoing brings us to, probably, the most difficult problem already signalled in the first section of this chapter, that is the problem of monetary policy under property rights structure in the economy in transition. It concerns the symbiotic relationship between state-owned ('nobody's') banks and state-owned ('nobody's') enterprises.

State banks do not look at their clients the way privately-owned banks do in the market economies. Historically they have been lending to large state-owned enterprises, and they continue to do s ), partly prodded by inertia, under the changed economic regime. Prudent lending policies, creditworthiness and risk assessment are not well known and even less cared for.

Lending inertia is matched by borrowing inertia. State enterprises are not very concerned about high debt-to-equity ratio, and they continue to borrow almost regardless of repayment capability. Especially the largest enterprises, historically least efficient and with the 'softest' budget constraint, are not deterred by any increase in the interest rate. They are sure that the state will bail them out from financial troubles as it did in the past.

The effect of the phenomenon in question on monetary policy is even worse than that of involuntary inter-enterprise credit. The latter weakens the impact of monetary restraint, while the former makes the effect perverse. As credit becomes dearer (and also often rationed) during the stabilization phase of the transition, the fact that largest and least efficient enterprises are able to borrow practically without limit reduces the access to credit for smaller and more efficient enterprises, both SOEs and private ones. Thus, restrictive monetary policy – contrary to textbook expectations – may result in adverse selection: survival of the least efficient and the demise of more efficient.

The logical recommendation stemming therefrom is to speed up privatization. Also logical is a suggestion to start with commercial banks, since there are so few of them relative to the number of industrial and other enterprises. But even the latter takes time, and in the meantime traditional monetary policy instruments should be supplemented by parallel measures correcting – to the largest extent possible – effects of lending and borrowing inertia.

Besides, it has been for quite some time not well appreciated that the privatization of banks has to be preceded by cleansing banks' balance sheets. And the latter could not be done without parallel looking into SOEs' bad loans inherited from the STE past. The issue is considered in the last, institutional section of the survey. Here it is worth signalling that only Czecho-Slovakia instituted some measures in this respect.

A problem of a different sort but also concerning monetary policy should also be mentioned at this point. It is not well recognized that monetary policy has an extremely potent impact on the level of economic activity, much beyond what one may observe in mature market economies of the West. This stems from the fact that state enterprises have entered the transition with a very low liquidity-to-output ratio. This has been, as has a very high inventories-to-output ratio, a legacy of the STE regime, where there were all the disincentives to keep the former ratio low. Therefore, a comparison with Western firms (to the extent that it is possible, given the shaky data base in post-STEs, shows strikingly large differences in current assets-to-fixed assets ratios in comparison with Western firms.

The consequence of the foregoing is that enterprise activity is highly sensitive to monetary policy changes. The transmission is also very fast: one or two months are sufficient for effects on output to become felt throughout the economy. Therefore marked shifts in monetary policy stance determine to a large extent output level in the short run.

Ominously, monetary policy has displayed much weaker impact on the price level. In all four countries, after initial fall from very high levels at the beginning of stabilization and liberalization programmes, inflation tends to persist everywhere, regardless of monetary policy stance. Interestingly, it has persisted regardless of the actual budgetary stance. More on inflation in the next section of this chapter.

Table 1.3 shows the budget balance of the general government in the countries covered by this survey. Everywhere fiscal policies have been successful at the start in balancing the budget, with increasing problems emerging afterwards. In Czecho-Slovakia balance was achieved even before the beginning of the transition programme, that is already in 1990. From January 1991, just as in Poland in 1990, the Czecho-Slovak budget has been recording ever-increasing surpluses (much larger than planned; see chapter 2). They peaked in May 1991 with 20.9 billion kcs, and – with some fiscal relaxation decided at mid-year – they began to decrease. In this Czecho-Slovak developments mirrored Polish ones a year later. There were differences, though. Czecho-Slovak government reduced the surplus somewhat faster, while in Poland this was achieved in the last few weeks of 1990 only; another difference was the size of the change in budgetary stance, as budget shifted from plus 20.9 billion kcs to minus 10 billion kcs in December 1991.

In Hungary the government planned a budget deficit to the tune of 78.8 billion Ft (after later upward adjustment), but the reality turned out to be worse and final deficit was 114 billion Ft. A characteristic feature of the foregoing has been that the increase in deficit was not the consequence of higher expenditures but that of lower revenues. This pattern seems to prevail everywhere in countries undergoing the

*Table 1.3* General government revenues (R), expenditures (E), and balance (B) in billion of units of national currency

|  | 1988 | 1989 | 1990 | 1991 |
|---|---|---|---|---|
| Czecho-Slovakia |  |  |  |  |
| R | 427.0 | 456.0 | 467.0 | . |
| E | 445.0 | 462.0 | 465.0 | . |
| B | −17.0 | −6.0 | 2.0 | −10.0 |
| Hungary |  |  |  |  |
| R | 706.3 | 836.8 | 1008.5 | . |
| E | 718.3 | 851.2 | 991.4 | . |
| B | −12.0 | −14.3 | 17.1 | −114.2 |
| Poland[a] |  |  |  |  |
| R | 10.1 | 30.1 | 196.2 | 210.9 |
| E | 10.0 | 33.7 | 193.8 | 241.9 |
| B | 0.1 | −3.6 | 2.4 | −31.0 |
| Yugoslavia |  |  |  |  |
| R | 4.7 | 60.8 | 477.4 | x |
| E | 4.6 | 66.6 | . | x |
| B | 0.1 | −5.8 | . | x |

*Note*: [a] Trillions

transition and nowhere was that more visible than in Poland.

Poland started the year 1991 with a balanced budget and plans for a very small budget deficit in 1990. The reality turned out to be much worse, though. Revenue shortfall forced the government to adjust the budget downward twice, and final 1991 figures were even lower than the lowest approved figures. Year-end deficit was 30.6 trillion zl. It is, however, not the size of the deficit *vis-à-vis* the GDP (still about 3 per cent) but the dramatically low level of expenditures (about 25 per cent) that endangered the performance of the budget sector, including that of the government itself. Prospects for 1992 are even bleaker in this respect for the maintenance of the existing very low level of budget expenditures requires much higher – and more dangerous inflation-wise – deficit.

The gist of the matter lies in the already signalled problem of the impact of the crisis of the SOEs' sector on the government budget.[6] Historical experience of countries undergoing stabilization suggests that the process of deficit reduction takes place rather slowly. But in post-STEs the pattern has been the reverse of that registered elsewhere. In country after country initial balancing of the budget took place almost overnight with surprising ease. However, usually in the second year of the stabilization programme, surplus turned into a deficit – and usually a fast growing one. Moreover, this growing deficit has been almost entirely due to the shortfall of revenues.

To explain the difference in balancing the budget between LDCs and post-STEs one should, as usual, look into the heritage of the post-STE regime and its impact upon the transition. State enterprises historically maintained large inventories of inputs. Accelerating inflation and aggravating disequilibria in the last years of the system accentuated the tendency.[7]

Now, the new rules of the game freed prices at which goods could be sold, while inputs to these products were bought earlier at much lower, controlled prices. Therefore, although output fell everywhere and capacity utilization was low, profitability was high.

Another heritage from the past has been the already mentioned very great dependence of the general government on revenues from the tax on profits of the enterprise sector. With SOEs' profitability remaining high on the one hand, and substantial cuts in subsidies on the other, budget balance was achieved rather fast. Over time, however, the gradual disappearance of windfall profits and continuing adverse effects, including the perverse ones, of monetary policy eroded SOEs' profitability, and revenues from that important source began to decrease.

In Hungary the impact has not been as strong as elsewhere because tax system reform has been accomplished earlier in that country. With a greater variety of taxes, including VAT and personal income tax already in place since 1988, even a drastic shortfall of revenues from one source was not as damaging as in Poland where profit tax played a much greater role as a revenue-earner for the Treasury. One may expect that in Czecho-Slovakia where profit tax on enterprises plays as great a role, serious problems may emerge in 1992, the second year of transition.

All countries so far tried to avoid re-igniting inflation by printing money. Therefore, they were generally adjusting their budgets downwards to keep deficits within manageable limits. An unintended consequence of these developments has been a fast decline of budget-to-GDP ratios (again, except Hungary, where the decline has been much less pronounced).

The difficulties analysed in the preceding paragraphs were aggravated by external factors as well. Countries in question additionally had to cope with the generally lower profitability resulting from recession, *inter alia* due to the collapse of the trade with the USSR.

In Poland and in Yugoslavia additional adverse contributions to the budget balance were made by policy-related factors. An unnecessarily renewed monetary squeeze from October 1990 to May 1991 contributed to stagnation and fall in output of the Polish economy and the resultant decline in profitability. The same happened in the pre-civil war Yugoslavia, where the impact of politically motivated monetary and fiscal relaxation by some constituent republics affected the budgetary process both directly and indirectly (through falling receipts).

Encouragingly, the process of reducing subsidies has been continuing everywhere, as shown in table 1.4. Everywhere the production subsidies have been initially reduced faster than consumption subsidies. The present writer expected in the earlier report that this trend might be broken in 1991 as the domestic effects of the collapse of the USSR trade would most probably force governments to adopt some stopgap support measures for the worst affected industries and enterprises.

This happened to some extent in Czecho-Slovakia, where subsidies to SOEs increased in nominal terms in relation to 1990 (although decreased in real terms). It did not happen in Poland, in spite of strong pressure on the government to that effect, only due to the disastrous state of the budget. The new government did promise a less stringent approach to the state sector, but again, given the state of the budget,

*Table 1.4*   Changes in relative size of subsidies (measured in per cent of GDP)

|                | 1988 | 1989 | 1990 | 1991 |
|----------------|------|------|------|------|
| Czecho-Slovakia | 13.0 | 16.0 | 12.1 | 7.0  |
| Hungary        | 13.4 | 9.1  | 8.4  | 6.0[a] |
| Poland         | 13.5 | 9.6  | 6.7  | 2.4  |
| Yugoslavia[b]  | 10.8 | 5.4  | .    | x    |

*Notes:* [a]rough estimate
[b]interventions in the economy resulting in budgetary expenditures

relief is expected to come largely through other channels (tax relief, easier credit and increased protection). Most cautious, as in many other respects, has been the approach to the problem in question in Hungary, where subsidies continue to decline in real terms, although at a relatively slow pace.

And finally, it should be kept in mind that the transition involves not only stabilization but also a shift to a freer economy. A part of this shift should also mean a reduced role for the state in redistributing resources through the state budget. Thus the transition implies the fall of the share of the budget in gross domestic product, although not quite in the way it happened in East Central Europe (the point is considered in the final section of this chapter, on institutional developments).

## PRICES, WAGES AND EMPLOYMENT

In all countries, except Czecho-Slovakia, the beginning of the transition took place in a highly inflationary environment (in Poland and Yugoslavia, in fact in the hyperinflationary environment). However, since stabilization has been only a part of transition programmes, price liberalization initially added to existing inflationary impulses. Therefrom stemmed significant jumps in the inflation rate in early 1990 in Poland and Yugoslavia and in early 1991 in Czecho-Slovakia. It is only in Hungary, which has been pursuing a more evolutionary stabilization programme, that the situation has been somewhat different. Although the present writer noted in the earlier report that in Hugary inflation has not decelerated so far on a year-to-year basis, data in the second part of table 1.5 reveal a significant slowdown on a monthly basis in the second half of 1991. Forecasts for 1992 all envisage a slower inflation rate, ranging between 20 and 25 per cent annually.

*Table 1.5* Inflation as measured by CPI

|  | Annual Rates | | | |
|---|---|---|---|---|
|  | *1988* | *1989* | *1990* | *1991* |
| Czecho-Slovakia | 0.2 | 1.4 | 10.0 | 57.9 |
| Hungary | 15.5 | 18.8 | 28.9 | 35.2 |
| Poland | 59.0 | 259.5 | 584.7 | 70.3 |
| Yugoslavia | 194.1 | 125.6 | 588.0 | x |

|  | 1991 Monthly Rates | | | | | | | | | | | |
|---|---|---|---|---|---|---|---|---|---|---|---|---|
|  | *Jan* | *Feb* | *Mar* | *Apr* | *May* | *Jun* | *Jul* | *Aug* | *Sep* | *Oct* | *Nov* | *Dec* |
| Czecho-Slovakia | 25.8 | 7.0 | 4.7 | 2.0 | 1.9 | 1.8 | −0.1 | 0.0 | 0.3 | −0.1 | 1.6 | 1.2 |
| Hungary | 7.5 | 4.4 | 3.5 | 2.4 | 2.2 | 2.1 | 0.9 | 0.2 | 1.5 | 1.3 | 1.4 | 1.6 |
| Poland | 12.7 | 6.7 | 4.5 | 2.7 | 2.7 | 4.9 | 0.1 | 0.6 | 4.3 | 3.2 | 3.2 | 3.1 |
| Yugoslavia | 4.9 | 9.0 | 3.2 | 5.0 | 10.9 | x | x | x | x | x | x | x |

Price liberalization reached a similar level everywhere, as some 85–90 per cent of all domestic prices were freed from (often ineffectual) controls. Another similarity concerned prices that remained in one way or another under central or local government control: they included fuel and electricity, housing maintenance and rent, postal and telecommunications services, and railway and other public transport services (a product group treated differently everywhere is pharmaceuticals).

Not for historical reasons alone, it is worth registering that the most extensive, most ineffectual – and therefore most often changed – were price regimes in Yugoslavia. For, given the history of ineffectual price controls, emerging countries may be burdened with the heritage of behavioural characteristics of economic agents that may in themselves be a hindrance to any stabilization effort.

What has been of primary importance in price developments is the fact that, in spite of the severity of monetary restraint and balanced budgets, inflation was not reduced, as expected by the architects of these programmes, to single digit level on an annual basis. Poland is probably the best example here. Since the abatement of hyperinflationary pressures and the effects of price liberalization of 1 January 1990, the inflation rate ranged (outliers apart) on the average of 3–4 per cent on a monthly basis. And this persistent inflation continued, regardless of whether the budget was in surplus, balance or deficit.

The country that seems to be closest to the one digit annual inflation target is in my opinion Czecho-Slovakia. Monthly data in the second part of table 1.4 show a very significant deceleration in the second half of 1991 in relation to the first. Four months of zero inflation up to October 1991 signifies something more than seasonal price decline due to the falling prices of agricultural produce experienced elsewhere. Also, price upswing afterwards has been much smaller than in the other countries of the region. To what extent this is an effect of macroeconomic restraint applied at the start of the transition in 1991 and to what extent it reflects the Czechs' and Slovaks' abhorrence of inflation and resultant cautiousness in setting prices and reacting to price increases, it remains to be seen. The depth of monetary restraint has not been in absolute terms greater than that in Poland in 1990, although it was more evenly applied over the year.

However, the generalized pattern of price increases in the face of falling demand implies the existence of many 'islands' of output concentration, not affected by increased foreign competition. Their monopolistic position allows them to raise prices. The fact that their profit margins tend often to fall rather than stay even does not invalidate the argument on the existence of monopolistic room for price increases, as, for example, Berg and Blanchard seem to suggest.[8]

There are few cases of the operation of a pure monopoly. Rather, we see in East Central Europe monopolists who try to combine price increases that absorb a certain part of cost increases with borrowing money to keep them going. The present writer has already analysed a certain built-in inertia stemming from the existing property rights structure. The symbiotic relationship between state banks and state enterprises supports inefficient or even unviable large enterprises through 'inertial' lending. Such policy may continue for quite some time before reaching the limit of tolerance of even the least prudent state banks.

A combination of factors associated with the transition process, with a deterioration in the external environment, together brought large declines in real wages and incomes of the population (for real wages, see table 1.6). Again, cross-country comparisons are no guide to the performance, since, for example, the fall in Czecho-Slovak real wages by 23.5 per cent (on September 1990–September 1991 basis) is comparable to the Polish fall in 1990 under similar circumstances. More revealing is a comparison between the real wage fall in Hungary by 7.5 per cent and the rise in Poland by about 2 per cent, for it shows

*Table 1.6*   Real wages: annually in percentage change

|  | 1988 | 1989 | 1990 | 1991 |
|---|---|---|---|---|
| Czecho-Slovakia | 2.1 | 0.8 | −5.8 | −23.5[a] |
| Hungary | [b] | −4.3 | −3.8 | −7.5[c] |
| Poland | 15.9 | −4.4 | −29.7 | 2.0[c] |
| Yugoslavia[b] | . | 14.0 | −22.0 | x |

*Notes:* [a]Jan–Sept 1991
　　　[b]Changes in wage calculations
　　　[c]Preliminary estimates

the stronger labour pressure and, plausibly, somewhat less prudent lending policies of Polish commercial banks.

At this point, however, a series of caveats has to be made, against oversimplified interpretations of the registered fall in standards-of-living-related indicators. First, most of the statistics registered under the Soviet-type economy are, as noted in the introduction, more or less distorted. Price, wage and income statistics belong to the most heavily distorted category. Generally, the hidden inflation overstates output and understates prices. The effect of understated prices is overstated real wages and incomes. Thus, the fall due to transition programmes is less steep, as its starts from a lower level than indicated by official statistics.

Second, in the case of standards-of-living comparisons, additional non-measurable distortions prevent unbiased comparisons across economic systems due to Soviet system-specific problems of shortages, forced substitution, low quality, etc. The shift to the market system that eliminates shortages almost overnight and increases the pressure to improve quality is improving welfare in a way that no conventional statistics are able to register.

Third, only a part of decline in real wages and incomes can be ascribed to the transition programmes and regarded as the 'costs of transition'. To the extent that macroeconomic restraint in the early phase of the transition programme aims at convincing economic agents that the transition is a decisive break with the past and not yet another half-hearted attempt, its wage and income consequences are really costs of the transition. But wage and income consequences of macroeconomic squeeze aimed at wringing out hyperinflation (as in Poland and Yugoslavia in 1990) are not transition costs. They would have been borne under any economic regime.

But returning for a moment to the 'costs of transition' issue, I would like to advance an important conclusion that, I think, emerges quite clearly from the recent transition experience of post STEs of East Central Europe. The credibility of transition, i.e. the task of convincing economic agents about its irreversibility, takes more time than has been, rather optimistically, expected. Therefore, the costs of macroeconomic restraint at the early phase of transition are not the only costs that will ultimately be borne by the societies in question.

Fourth, if pre-transition figures are overstated, then transition figures tend to be understated. They are collected in larger, generally state-owned enterprises, usually excluding most of the private sector, where registered wages tend to be higher. To the extent that they cover a part of the latter, they understate the wage level and rate of increase anyway. Since the whole remuneration is not registered (a common phenomenon in private firms) it is not captured by the coverage.

It is worth mentioning in the context of the 'costs of transition' issue, that in all four countries some form of wage control has been instituted, and in those countries that started earlier it was maintained in 1991 as well. Although the efficiency of these measures is seen even by their supporters as being rather low, it continues to be preferred by international institutions recommending a standardized stabilization programme.

Labour markets in countries under consideration have continued to undergo major changes in many respects. The most visible, of course, has been the continuous rise in unemployment (see table 1.7). The process continued and even accelerated in 1991 as competitive and other pressures forced many SOEs to shed labour. The discrepancy between larger declines of output and smaller declines of employment suggest, however, the potential for further redundancies.

What is also worth noticing with respect to unemployment, is the

*Table 1.7*    Unemployment (end-of-the-year data; absolute figures in thousands)

|  | 1988 | 1989 | 1990 | 1991 |
|---|---|---|---|---|
| Czecho-Slovakia | 0 | 0 | 77 | 524 |
| Hungary | 0 | 12 | 80 | 406[a] |
| Poland | 0 | 10 | 1126 | 2156 |
| Yugoslavia[b] | 1132 | 1201 | 1308 | 1489[b] |

*Notes:* [a]End-of-September 1991
        [b]End-of-June 1991

fact that most redundancies have so far been the result of trimming down employment within enterprises. There have been very few bankruptcies (some reasons for such patterns of unemployment have been advanced earlier in the survey, see the third section of this chapter). The fact that many unviable enterprises continue to operate makes the potential for decrease in employment in the state sector larger still in all countries in question.

On the other hand, present employment and unemployment statistics most certainly understate the level of employment and – often grossly – overstate unemployment. First, statistics generally cover only the state sector, where employment has been declining everywhere. Recent improvements in the coverage, such as those in Hungary for example, include all enterprises employing above a certain threshold (in Hungary, 50 persons). In consequence they register only a fraction of employment in the private sector, while the numerically dominant remainder is only estimated.

Besides, employment in the private sector, large or small, is certainly grossly understated. Understated figures stem largely from two different sources. First, registered firms, especially smaller ones, understate the level of employment. A Hungarian source 'guesstimated' that for one registered employed, 4–10 unregistered employees work in private firms.[9] Even if the guesstimate in question is on the high side, it strongly underlines the markedly higher level of employment in the registered private sector. Second, given the history of post-STEs in transition, there exists a large unregistered, informal private sector, not counted under any regular statistical surveys or estimates.

Thus, the level of employment is markedly higher than the one registered by the still maladapted labour statistics. The obverse of the phenomenon in question is a no less markedly lower unemployment level. The realistic rate of unemployment is anybody's guess. But instead of attempting yet another guesstimate, the present writer suggests an alternative assessment. Large centres of economic activity may be regarded as practically unemployment-free (apart from really frictional ones). What matters – and matters a lot – is unemployment in smaller towns and in the countryside. Particularly acute is the problem in one-employer cities that depended not only for employment but also for many otherwise municipality-delivered services on one bankrupt firm.

## EXCHANGE RATE REGIMES AND POLICIES, FOREIGN
## TRADE AND CURRENT ACCOUNT PERFORMANCE

It is in this particular area that the performance has been most satisfactory in East Central European transition. Foreign exchange regimes were liberalized, and limited convertibility (more or less limited convertibility on current account) has been maintained everywhere, except in Yugoslavia (see p.27). Foreign trade performance has been surprisingly good, even if the pattern was atypical, and current account figures were also better than expected. Furthermore, Czecho-Slovakia, Hungary and Poland weathered the shock associated with the shift to convertible currency trade with the USSR with less deficit than forecasted – and that in spite of the fact that the shock effects turned out to be stronger.

As stressed in the preceding paragraph, all economies in transition liberalized their foreign exchange regimes. The term 'internal convertibility' used in all countries except Yugoslavia has, however, somewhat different content in each case. In Poland it means the right to acquire unlimited amounts of convertible currencies at an established exchange rate by all domestic economic agents, enterprises and households, and the right of the latter to maintain bank accounts denominated in foreign currencies. Since the passage of the amended foreign investment bill by Polish parliament in June 1991, foreigners are allowed to convert profits and wages earned in Poland in zlotys into foreign currencies and repatriate them to their countries of domicile. Other currency conversions by foreigners, such as exchanging otherwise obtained zlotys into foreign currencies are not allowed (albeit this is difficult to enforce).

In Hungary enterprises have the same rights as in Poland, but households' right to purchase foreign currencies is limited. The repatriation of profits earned in Hungary by foreigners has already been allowed under Hungarian law earlier on. In Czecho-Slovakia limits on households' rights to buy foreign currencies are more stringent than in Hungary. Moreover, there are some administrative constraints put on enterprises as well, such as the duty to consult the respective commercial bank in the case of large scale imports.

For these reasons, in both countries in question black market exchange rates did not disappear overnight as they did in Poland. Nonetheless, given the foreign trade performance, the differential between official fixed (or, more precisely, pegged) exchange rates and black market ones has been narrowing over time. The data confirming this are shown in table 1.8.

*Table 1.8* Exchange rates *vis-à-vis* $ (annual averages in units of national currency)

|  | 1988 | 1989 | 1990 | 1991 |
|---|---|---|---|---|
| Czecho-Slovakia |  |  |  |  |
| Official | 14.36 | 15.05 | 17.39 | 29.48 |
| Unofficial | 33.44 | 42.39 | (39.0–40.0) | 32.28 |
| Hungary |  |  |  |  |
| Official | 50 | 59 | 63 | 74 |
| Unofficial | . | . | . | . |
| Poland |  |  |  |  |
| Official | 431 | 1446 | 9500 | 10559 |
| Unofficial | 1979 | 5565 | 9570 | 10731 |

Full convertibility on current account has been introduced in Yugoslavia at the originally realistic exchange rate in December 1989 as part of a stabilization-cum-liberalization programme. This generated the surge of westbound exports in early 1990. However, the vagaries of macroeconomic policy resulted in higher than expected inflation in the second half of 1990 that made the dinar increasingly overvalued, generating in turn an enormous import surge in the fourth quarter of 1990 and $4.6 billion trade deficit for 1990 as a whole. The dinar had to be devalued on 1 January 1991, and convertibility has been first strongly circumscribed, and later – under the strains of civil strife – suspended. Independent republics have been trying of late to establish convertibility of their new currencies (such as the Slovin tolar).

Good foreign trade performance on convertible currency markets in general and the pattern of trade in convertible currencies after the start of transition in particular merit special attention in the survey. The rationale for the attention is that it has not only explanatory but also predictive value, as far as other post-STEs entering that path are concerned. The second, no less important, reason is that it highlights the harmful role of fixed exchange rate as an 'anchor' of the standardized stabilization programme.

The generalized trade pattern under internal and external liberalization has been well described in the literature.[10] Once liberalization reveals the real pattern of comparative advantages, export expansion is expected to follow. However, the process of finding export markets takes more time than that of sending orders abroad for goods that were not permitted earlier under exchange and trade controls. Therefore, import surge precedes export surge in every liberalization.

And this is also a rationale behind the establishment of stabilization funds set up under the aegis of the IMF that were supposed to help post-STEs in transition to withstand the pressures on foreign exchange reserves in the interim period between the start of the transition and the expected export expansion.

But the reverse was the case in East Central Europe. Stabilization funds were left unutilized, as in country after country export surge started rather quickly following the beginning of the transition. In the only country it did not, that is in Czecho-Slovakia, the fall in imports was initially larger than that in exports. Thus, also in this last case there was no need to draw upon a stabilization facility.

Annual trade data in table 1.9 do not well reflect the phenomenon but the pattern was an export surge followed rather than preceded by import surge. The answer to that puzzle is found in the heritage of the STE-regime combined with the harmful impact of exchange rate treated as a stabilization 'anchor'.[11]

State enterprises under the STE regime display a marked tendency to hoard both inputs and production factors. Data show that the inventory-to-output ratios there are very much higher than in market economies. A substantial part of hoarded inputs and capital goods are imports. The pressure for imports, especially imports from the West, is even stronger than that for domestic products. It is understandable. On the one hand their quality (including technological sophistication) is generally better, delivery times shorter, while on the other the price under standard price equalization schemes is the same. And even if it is not, the 'soft' budget constraint makes SOEs much less, if at all, concerned about price differentials.

Once transition begins and the demand fall described earlier (see the section on output patterns above) takes place, part of that fall also affects imported inputs and capital goods. First, SOEs now have incentives to reduce oversized inventories of the already obtained imports and, second, they also now look differently at price differentials. It is not import availability, as in the past, but price vs. quality differential that matter. Furthermore, the impact of initial macroeconomic restraint on output reinforces the decline of import orders. Therefrom stems the initial import fall in post-STEs in transition. Although the impact of recession is well understood, the impact of systemic change is not.

*Table 1.9* Exports (E), imports (I), and trade balance (B) with the West (in million of $)

|  | 1988 | 1989 | 1990 | 1991 |
|---|---|---|---|---|
| *Czecho-Slovakia* | | | | |
| E: West's data | 4040 | 4390 | 5020 | . |
| E: Nat. data | 4580 | 4970 | 5610 | 6779 |
| I: West's data | 4010 | 3970 | 5340 | . |
| I: Nat. data | 4940 | 4870 | 6050 | 6748 |
| B: West's data | 30 | 420 | −320 | . |
| B: Nat. data | −360 | 100 | −440 | 51 |
| *Hungary* | | | | |
| E: West's data | 4220 | 4700 | 5860 | . |
| E: Nat. data | 4310 | 4640 | 5570 | 6506 |
| I: West's data | 4160 | 4870 | 5500 | . |
| I: Nat. data | 4340 | 4690 | 4750 | 6504 |
| B: West's data | 60 | −170 | 360 | . |
| B: Nat. data | −30 | −50 | 820 | 2 |
| *Poland* | | | | |
| E: West's data | 5870 | 6340 | 8740 | . |
| E: Nat. data | 6480 | 6800 | 9200 | 14218 |
| I: West's data | 5210 | 6430 | 7100 | . |
| I: Nat. data | 5900 | 6410 | 5860 | 14247 |
| B: West's data | 660 | −90 | 1640 | . |
| B: Nat. data | 580 | 390 | 3340 | −29 |
| *Yugoslavia* | | | | |
| E | 9624 | 10519 | 11834 | x |
| I | 10202 | 11971 | 16504 | x |
| B | −578 | −1452 | −4670 | x |

A closer look at post-STEs in early transition period signals that import surge did materialize. In the opinion of the present writer this need not have been the case and the blame for the surge should be put on the architects and implementors of the standardized stabilization programmes. Fixed exchange rates used as nominal 'anchors' proved to be incompatible with the smooth shift to export orientation based on comparative advantages. The point made here is not completely new; it has already been made, e.g., with respect to Chile.[12]

Benefits of opening up, or export orientation, come in two intellectually very distinct (but practically overlapping) phases. Phase one is relatively short and associated with the removal of most of the foreign trade control and the initial devaluation of domestic currency to make the exchange rate realistic. Domestic producers realize quickly that selling abroad may bring higher profits. The result is an increase in exports from existing capacities and under the unchanged structure of production factors. This is what happened in Yugoslavia and Poland in 1990 after the start of respective transition programmes and, to some extent, in Hungary under further trade liberalization and exchange rate adjustment in the same year.

But phase one is only the beginning of a lasting reorientation. As comparative advantages are revealed, some goods become lastingly more profitable to export than others. In consequence, a shift of production factors from less profitable to more profitable export-oriented branches and product groups occurs in liberalizing economies. However, for the foregoing to take place, real exchange rates should stay reasonably stable. It is at this point that the harmful role of an exchange rate as an anti-inflationary 'anchor' reveals itself.

As fixed exchange rate is used that way, the policy bias is to maintain exchange rate pegged for too long. In the extreme case of Poland, after initial (large) devaluation, the exchange rate remained unchanged for 17 months, during which prices rose by about 330 per cent. On a quarter-by-quarter basis this meant an 81.2 per cent appreciation of zloty (still more on a month-by-month basis). The result was a steep loss of competitiveness.

Effects on the trade pattern were dramatic. In the first half of 1990 exports amounted to 119.7 per cent of those in the first half of 1989, while imports were only 54.1 per cent. In 1990 as a whole exports rose to 140 per cent of those in 1989, while imports already exceeded those of the preceding year (106.3 per cent). But in the first three quarters of 1991 exports were 117.9 per cent of those in the equivalent period of 1990, while imports rose by a whopping 196.5%. The same happened in Yugoslavia in 1990 where the defence of the dinar pegged to the DM resulted in the enormous import surge in the last quarter of 1990 (with forced devaluation afterwards).

In Hungary overvaluation appeared much more slowly. Nonetheless, between the second quarter of 1990 and the first quarter of 1991 the forint rose *vis-à-vis* the US $ by 20.3 per cent[13]. Foreign trade results showed that clearly enough: in 1990 exports amounted to 131 per cent of those in 1989 and imports were 112 per cent. In the first half of 1991 the respective figures were 127 per cent and 177 per cent.

As a result, benefits of the second phase of export orientation did not materialize, or were thoroughly weakened. With overvaluation super-seding initial undervaluation, production factors did not, on the whole, shift to the more profitable export sector for the very reason that this sector has been rapidly or slowly losing its higher profitability. Partial corrections made on an *ad hoc* basis did not help much and the credibility of the much talked about structural change in favour of the export-oriented sector has been thoroughly undermined.

One of the real problems post-STEs in transition face in common is the choice of a sensible exchange rate regime that would not add to inflation *per se* and at the same time would ensure real exchange rate stability based on predictability of nominal exchange rate changes. The history of stabilization programmes following hyperinflationary episodes does not include a case where the inflation rate fell to one digit level in a time span shorter than half a decade to a full decade. Therefore, for the interim period other choices than pegged exchange rate are preferable.

The present writer favours a tablita-like exchange rate adjustable at short, regular intervals but, differently from tablita, with the adjustment rule of 90 per cent accommodation of inflation differentials between a transition country and its main trading partners. On the one hand it would apply some pressure to reduce costs on domestic producers, while on the other it would make changes more predictable. Moreover, it would prevent sudden import surges that not only upset the outward orientation but also generate protectionist sentiments.

Before shifting attention to post-COMECON trade, one matter needs emphasizing: the fact that under such a roller coaster exporters performed as well as they did is a proof not only of the stimulating role of initial devaluations but also of the fact that, to some degree, adjustment did take place in the state sector. That it was not more marked is the result of both perverse effects of monetary policy (analysed in the section above on monetary and fiscal policies) and a wrong choice of the exchange rate regime.

In 1991 non-convertible currency trade (in transferable roubles) has been only a small carry-over residual of the once dominant non-convertible currency trade within the now extinct COMECON. The shift to convertible currency trade with the Soviet Union at the beginning of 1991 brought about, as expected, a larger fall in exports to the USSR than imports (mostly fuels) from that country. The fall of exports became generally even larger than expected. This put very strong strains on the level of economic activity in Czecho-Slovakia, Hungary and Poland (and to a lesser extent Yugoslavia). A Polish government assessment ascribed 62.7 per cent of the fall in industrial output in January–April 1991 to direct and indirect consequences of the fall in exports to the USSR and other ex-COMECON countries. Another, foreign study puts the figure at 25–50 per cent of the fall for the first half of 1991.[14] In the case of Hungary and Czechoslovakia assessments show even larger shares of the total fall.[15]

Incidentally, the whole issue of transition from non-convertible to convertible currency trade with the USSR has been grossly mismanaged by Soviet economic decision-makers. Being under increased pressure due to the fast deteriorating domestic economy, they decided to improve the situation by cutting implied subsidies to their fuels and raw material exports to ex-COMECON partners. The calculation was that they would run large convertible currency surpluses with the latter countries, which could subsequently be used to increase imports from the West.

Surpluses materialized indeed, but turned out to be much smaller due to lower orders (as well as to the inability of the USSR to deliver contracted quantities). But cuts in imports from ex-COMECON economies backfired. Some shifting of orders for consumer goods to the West did occur, but Soviet planners forgot that their factories were producing technologically obsolete goods for which inputs are simply unavailable in the West any more (as they ceased to be manufactured decades ago). This created multiple supply bottlenecks in Soviet enterprises, with missing East European supplies contributing substantially to the general fall in industrial output registered in the USSR.

Once this has been recognized, some attempts have been made (on both sides) partly to restore fast declining trade so as to give enterprises time to adjust. However, the dramatic developments since the failed communist putsch of August 1991 added to turbulence in trade relations. The fact that under the circumstances both trade and current account balances deteriorated less than expected, or even turned positive, has been mostly due to relatively successful westward trade reorientation of these economies.

## INSTITUTIONAL DEVELOPMENTS

The year 1991 witnessed the continuation of institutional changes in the countries concerned, with the unhappy exception of Yugoslavia. The disintegration of Yugoslavia first halted changes in constituent republics and later shifted efforts from ex-federal to the level of now independent (or attempting at independence) republics. It should probably be said at the outset that, in spite of strenuous efforts, supply of institutional infrastructure has been much too low relative to the demands of the 'workable' market economy, let alone the efficient one. The gap may diminish only with time – and further efforts at closing the gap through the passage of many rules, whose absence limits the benefits of the liberalization programmes now in operation.

Apart from setting certain basic rules, from commercial codes to accounting principles, three areas have been in the strongest need of greater institutional effort: the development of financial markets, privatization and tax reform. As it turned out, rather belatedly, the latter – a cornerstone of the 'workable' market economy – is difficult if not impossible to achieve without the former. At a certain stage separate efforts have to be put together to achieve the desired change. On the other hand, the generally neglected changes in the inherited tax system made a strong comeback to the centre of decision-makers' attention, as excessive dependence on some taxes strongly and adversely affected the stream of tax revenues collected by the state.

Development of the financial markets proceeded in Czecho-Slovakia, Hungary and Poland in 1991 along roughly parallel lines, as far as the banking system is concerned. But Czecho-Slovakia went ahead of the other two with respect to the increasingly important issue of cleansing banks' portfolios from the heritage of the past.

One of the serious obstacles everywhere in economies in transition has been the presence of many doubtful or outrightly non-collectible loans in commercial banks' portfolios. Banks that perceived the shakiness of their portfolios have been charging excessive interest rates on credits to good performers, affecting adversely the level of economic activity.

A peculiarity of the Czecho-Slovak situation was the provision of permanently revolving credits to SOEs for the maintenance of overly large inventories with no maturity dates (*sic!*). The Federal government created a new institution: the Consolidation Bank, that has taken over these loans to the tune of kcs 50 billion (about one tenth of all outstanding loans to state enterprises). These loans will be refinanced with eight-year maturities and an interest rate of 13 per cent. But even this cleansing of balances was not enough, as banks still carry many doubtful loans and at the same time are seriously undercapitalized (very low capital adequacy ratios of 1–2 per cent). Such a situation makes them the unlikely candidates for the urgently needed privatization. Therefore, other measures aiming at the improvement of banks' positions, both strengthening the capital base and improving loans' portfolios, will be the priority in the future.

In Hungary the two-tier banking system had been formally introduced in 1987. Since then a few dozen banking institutions have been established. Nonetheless, old state-owned commercial banks represent slightly less than 90 per cent of the total share capital of the banking system (incidentally, this ratio roughly holds for Czechoslovakia and Poland as well).

So far, no efforts have been made either in Hungary or in Poland to tackle the problem of shaky portfolios of old, state-owned commercial banks. The issue seems to have been of particular urgency in Poland, where, however, the proposal made before the elections to start the interaction of debtors and creditors (state banks and SOEs) did not catch the attention of decision-makers,[16] while the government's schemes are in need of external support that is not forthcoming, given the perceived deficiencies of the schemes themselves.

Everywhere there emerge new, mostly privately-owned banks. There are already a few dozen of them in each of the three countries: Czecho-Slovakia, Hungary and Poland. Most are very small, undercapitalized and therefore extremely cautious in their operations. Collaterals exceeding 100 per cent of the loan are not an uncommon requirement in these banks, which makes them lombard-like institutions rather than banks. Since large state-owned banks do not base their loan decisions on the riskiness of submitted projects and creditworthiness of firms (see the second section of this chapter), the banking system in post-STEs does not play its basic allocative role in a minimally satisfactory manner.

So far only in Hungary have these deficiencies been alleviated to some, still not very large extent by the emergence of banks with mixed Hungarian/foreign ownership, subsidiaries of foreign banks and other financial institutions. Western banks are very cautious in East Central Europe, and rarely go beyond establishing a representative's office. Nowhere is this cautiousness more in evidence than in Poland. The reasons are both bank-specific and country-specific at the same time. Poland is the only country of the three that demanded renegotiation of its debt to foreign banks (grouped in the London Club), and also is seen as a greater risk due to more politically charged economic debates at the country level.

It should be noted that revealed deficiencies of the banking system will not be compensated by such visible changes as the opening of the

Polish stock market in Warsaw in the spring of 1991 or the forthcoming opening of the Czecho-Slovak one. The existence of stock-markets in Budapest and Warsaw has so far been little more than a useful educational device with much better prospects for the more distant future.

Another institutional area of crucial importance is privatization. Many of the liberalizing measures undertaken at the beginning of the transition will not bear fruits of greater efficiency before private property rights reduce the exorbitant agency costs characteristic of state ownership. Weak performance of post-STEs is directly related to the fact that what was achieved so far has been, however inadvertently, an institutional set-up defined as market socialism: market institutions plus dominant state ownership.

In the countries in question privatization proceeded throughout 1991 in many different ways. In Hungary and Poland it was the continuation of efforts, including regulatory ones, that started earlier. But in Czecho-Slovakia it was only in February 1991 that the two landmark privatization bills were passed by the Federal Parliament laying down foundations for the change in the property rights structure.

One problem began to emerge as crucial in relation to privatization activities, namely the issue of enterprises that will not be privatized in the short run. However sensible is the idea that private owners know better than bureaucrats how to restructure an acquired enterprise, it does not address the issue of those enterprises, which for one reason or another will not be privatized within the next year or two. Privatization everywhere turned out to be a more drawn out affair than optimists imagined and the issue of enterprises left adrift became a matter of increasing urgency.

However reluctantly, it has been recognized that if matters of restructuring are left to SOEs themselves, very little pre-privatization restructuring will be done. Furthermore, if left to managers and workers, there will be, over time, less and less to restructure, as many inefficient SOEs' are eating themselves up, covering current costs with revenues from asset sales.[17] However, little more has come out of that recognition so far, apart from the determination to proceed faster through various privatization paths. The importance of the issue is nonetheless such that it may become one of the main privatization concerns of 1992 in both Hungary and Poland.

In Czecho-Slovakia the answer so far has been the iron determination to proceed as fast as possible with mass privatization through the voucher system that, supported by sale to foreign investors and by public floating, would dispose of some 85 per cent of state-owned industrial assets in two years. The year 1992 will put this strategy to a decisive test. The year 1991 was a period of preparation and the end of the year, as well as early 1992, revealed how much the whole voucher programme depended on unforeseen developments, originally deemed to be of marginal importance. This author has in mind the meteoric rise of public interest in mass privatization after the appearance of (largely unregulated) mutual funds that bid aggressively for people's vouchers. If core shareholders do not emerge in a year or two from now in enterprises privatized through the voucher method, the problem in question now afflicting Polish and Hungarian SOEs may return in a more acute form (and may be on a larger scale as well).

In Czecho-Slovakia, Hungary and Poland a number of large enter-prises were privatized through the sale of substantial or majority stakes to foreign firms, the largest being the Skoda–Volkswagen deal. In the case of some oligopolistically structured industries we have witnessed a chain reaction across East Central Europe caused by the rivalry characteristic of such markets. Once one of these firms was known to have acquired an equity stake in a local producer, other firms entered the race buying into local firms as well. This has been happening, for example, in the motor and the soap and cosmetics industries. On the whole, however, foreign investments other than small scale/high risk ventures have been relatively rare (that is relative to over-optimistic expectations in these countries). What should be signalled here is an asymmetric location of foreign investments there, with more than half of all investments in the region as a whole going to Hungary.

A brief overview of other privatization paths seems in order here. In contrast with the Czecho-Slovak mass privatization scheme, the Polish one, unveiled in 1991, fared much worse. It was rejected by the outgoing parliament and remained in limbo until the new Polish government declared its intention to move fast in this direction.

In Czecho-Slovakia the so-called 'small privatization' (i.e. auction sale or lease of shops, restaurants, pharmacies, building sites) started successfully on 1 January 1991. By the end of December 1991, almost 20,000 different economic units had been sold bringing 23.3 billion kcs to the treasury. This process began earlier in Hungary and con-tinued, albeit more slowly than expected, and more slowly than in Czecho-Slovakia or Poland, throughout 1991. At the end of December some 2,100 shops and restaurants were sold or leased (out of 9,600 slated for privatization). 'Small privatization' has been most rapid in Poland where, according to the most recent statistics, almost three quarters of all state-owned shops and restaurants have been privatized. The ownership structure did not change significantly, though. For only 1–2 per cent of all privatized shops were actually sold; the remaining 98–99 per cent were leased only.

The government of Hungary, which had been resisting any type of free distribution of state property, has recognized more recently the need to speed up the privatization process. Prodded by the criticism coming from different directions, the State Property Agency decided to initiate a 'fast-track' procedure for smaller firms with fewer than 300 employees. The scheme will include about 350 companies. The speed is to be achieved through the simplified procedure only; market price has to be arrived at through the competitive bidding process.

The previous Polish government also discovered a fast-track privatization procedure: privatization through liquidation. In the first half of 1991, 333 enterprises, usually smaller ones (although no size limit has been set), obtained the liquidation decision. There is a snag here, too. In about half of the cases assets were not sold but leased to employees. Economic theory is unambiguous in its negative evaluation of the efficiency of leasing arrangements. On top of it, collective leasing is even more inefficient, as it entails the emergence of a 'free rider' problem. However, this privatization path turned out to be the most productive one in numerical terms.

As it was originally seen as a very particular path of marginal importance, it has been yet another lesson (after recent developments in Czecho-Slovakia with regard to the voucher scheme) of the Hayekian dictum, that economic agents (and economists) cope with the inevitable ignorance. It has also been a lesson in the role of the competitive process that ultimately will decide on the most efficient solution – this time for privatization. Putting all the eggs in one basket, however appealing, forecloses all other options and exposes the country to a much higher risk than under the application of 'Brzeski rule' (a problem-specific application of Hayekian principle), that is, trying every possible form of privatization at once.[18]

Ownership transformation of the state sector is only a part of the change in ownership structure. It may be called privatization 'from above'. No less important is the privatization 'from below', that is the establishment and expansion of new private firms. Here fundamental laws on entrepreneurship were passed everywhere before 1991.

However, the institution-building in the case of privatization 'from below' does not – or should not – end there. To ensure their successful growth to minimum efficient scale, a whole network of small business-oriented banks, credit unions, rural financial co-operatives, insurance companies geared to servicing high-risk small businesses, venture capital institutions, innovation and management centres ought to emerge.

Regretfully, in no country under consideration has institutional support for the private small business sector received the attention it deserves. And yet without these institutions the size structure of these economies will never approach that of market economies, where healthy small and medium-sized firms constitute a backbone of the national economy.

It should also be obvious that some of the problems encountered by privatization stem from the underdeveloped financial markets. Their underdevelopment is strongly in evidence with respect to servicing the private sector. Privatization by successful domestic businessmen often fails due to the lack of credit available to those willing to buy the state enterprises who may need credits to cover some 50–75 per cent of the bidding price.

The foregoing points to yet another institution that should be created but so far has not been in either country, namely a privàtization bank. By extending credits solely for the purpose of purchasing state assets, mortgaged on these very assets, it would speed up the privatization process and at the same time link privatization 'from below.' with that 'from above'. Another benefit of such a privatization bank is the improvement of the size structure of the economy. For private entre-preneurs would be free to exercise their judgement on the desirability of maintaining SOE as a going concern, merging it with their earlier businesses, hiving off parts they deem to be unsuitable for their needs, etc. The 'right' size, based on profitability criteria, would thus emerge more efficiently than through the process of the breaking up of large SOEs based on a bureaucratic fiat (as was the case in Hungary).

Regardless of the difficulties, however, it is privatization 'from below' that has made greatest strides so far. In Hungary the share of the private sector in the national economy increased from about 10 per cent to almost 30 per cent.[19] In Poland, where agriculture remained largely private for most of the communist period, it was about 30 per cent at the start of the transition in 1989. But outside agriculture the change has been no slower than in Hungary and the share of the private sector no smaller, either. Toward the end of 1991 a share of private sector's output was some 22.5–25 per cent in industry, about 45 per cent in construction, 16–18 per cent in transportation, about 75 per cent in retail trade, etc. And if one adds the informal sector, the share of private ownership will be even larger.

Both countries were certainly well advanced along the road leading to a 'mixed' economy. Even if this is not a target social reformers in those countries had in mind, as an interim goal for the mid-1990s it is good enough. For it shows the road travelled already by these economies: from one end of the ownership spectrum towards its mid-point. The attainment of the 'mixed' economy status also promises more efficient performance, as the impact of privately-owned firms will undoubtedly make its mark on the performance of the economy as a whole.

Finally, although it is often debated in general terms in East Central Europe that the role of the state in the economy should be strongly circumscribed, very little is being said about cutting the state budget to size in line with such requirements. Only in the Czecho-Slovak economic leadership there seems to be an explicitly stated determination to cut the budget/GDP ratio. Determination apart, 1991 witnessed a drastic fall in that ratio in Poland not by design but more or less as a by-product of macroeconomic developments analysed in the third section of this chapter. In Hungary the reduction of the budget-to-GDP ratio proceeds much more slowly and from a much higher level.

But there is a sea of difference between shifting various activities 'traditionally' financed through the state budget to the private sector and their disappearance as a result of the acute shortage of funds. At the time of writing this was, however, the reality in the Poland of 1991 and may become a problem of similar proportions in Czecho-Slovakia in 1992 due to the similarity in the inherited tax system.

## NOTES

1  See, *inter alia*, J. Winiecki, 'The Polish Transition Programme at Mid-1991: Stabilisation under Threat, Kieler Diskussionsbeiträge 174, Institut für Weltwirtschaft, Kiel, September 1991; *Occasional Paper No. 3*, Adam Smith Research Centre, Warsaw, 1991; *idem*, 'The Transition of Post-Soviet-Type Economies: Expected and Unexpected Developments', *Banca Nazionale del Lavoro Quarterly Review*, no. 181, June 1992; *idem*, 'Monetary perversity in Post-Soviet Economies', *Wall Street Journal*, 2 February 1992.

2  See J. Kornai's classic book on the subject, *Economics of Shortage*, North
   Holland, Amsterdam, 1980; *idem*, 'Soft Budget Constraint', *Kyklos*, vol.
   39, no. 1, 1986.
3  See J. Winiecki, 'The Polish Transition Programme at Mid-1991'.
4  See J. Winiecki, 'The Transition of Post-Soviet-type Economies'; *idem*,
   'Walesa Must Resist the "Reflation" Siren Song', *Wall Street Journal*, 21
   December 1990; *idem* 'The Inevitability of a Fall in Output in the Early
   Stages of Transition to the Market', *Soviet Studies*, vol. 43, no. 4.
5  Data from K. Dyba and J. Svejnar, 'Stabilization and Transition in
   Czechoslovakia', NBER Conference on Transition in Eastern Europe,
   Cambridge, Mass. 26–29 February 1992. M. Hrncir, 'Transition to a Market
   Economy: The Case of the CSFR' Paper prepared for a Kiel Week
   Conference on The Transformation of Socialist Economies, Kiel, 26–28
   June 1991, gives somewhat different figures for the earlier period.
6  See earlier explanations in J. Winiecki, 'The Transition of Post-Soviet-type
   Economies'; *idem*, 'Monetary Perversity in Post-Soviet-Type Economies',
   *Wall Street Journal*, 6 February 1992; *idem*, *Polish Transition Programme:
   Underpinnings, Results, Interpretations*, Stockholm School of Economics,
   February 1992.
7  See, e. g., from the USSR, G. Popov and N. Shmelev, *The Turning Point:
   Revitalizing the Soviet Economy*, Doubleday, New York, 1989 and J.
   Winiecki, 'The Transition of Post-Soviet-type Economies'.
8  A. Berg and O. Blanchard, 'Stabilization and transition in Poland
   1990–1991', NBER Conference on Transition in Eastern Europe, Cam-
   bridge, Mass., 26–29 February 1992.
9  See, *Barometer of Privatization*, 91/1, Budapest, October 1991, p. 15.
10 See, in particular, A. O. Krueger, *Foreign Trade Regimes and Economic
   Development*, Ballinger, Cambridge, Mass., 1978; *idem* 'Trade Policy as
   Input to Development', *American Economic Review*, vol. 70, no. 2, May
   1980, pp. 288–92; J. N. Bhagwati, *Anatomy and Consequences of Exchange
   Control Regimes*, Ballinger, Cambridge, Mass., 1978; B. Balassa, *The
   Newly Industrializing Countries in the World Economy*, Pergamon Press,
   London, 1981; and B. Balassa and others, *Development Strategies in
   Semi-industrial Economies*, Johns Hopkins University Press, Baltimore,
   1982.
11 On the former explanation see in particular J. Winiecki, 'Central Planning
   and Export Orientation', *Oeconomica Polona*, 1983, nos. 3–4 *idem*,
   'Central Planning and Export Orientation in Manufactures (Theoretical
   considerations on the impact of system-specific features on specialisation)',
   *Economic Notes*, 1985, no. 2 on foreign trade characteristics; *idem*,
   'Distorted Macroeconomics of Central Planning', *Banca Nazionale del
   Lavoro Quarterly Review*, June 1986, no. 157; J. Kornai, *Growth, Efficiency
   and Shortage*, Blackwell, Oxford, 1982, on hoarding.
12 See S. Edwards, 'Stabilization and Liberalization Policies in Eastern
   Europe: Lessons from Latin America', in *The Emergence of Market
   Economies in Eastern Europe*, ed. C. Clague and G. Rausser, Blackwell,
   Oxford, 1992.

13 Real exchange rate indices on quarterly basis taken from D. Rodrik, 'Foreign trade in Eastern Europe's transition: early results', NBER Conference on Transition in Eastern Europe, Cambridge, Mass., 26–29 February 1992.

14 The respective studies are *Information on Economic Conditions in the First Half of 1991 with Elements of a Forecast*, Central Planning Bureau, Warsaw, 25 July 1991 (in Polish) and A. Berg and O. Blanchard *Stabilisation and Transition*.

15 See D. Rodrik, 'Foreign trade in Eastern Europe's transition'.

16 See 'Letter to the President' by four economists, J. Beksiak, U. Grzelonska, T. M.Rybczynski and J. Winiecki, in *Rzeczpospolita* 15 and 16 October 1991.

17 See 'Falling Value of State Companies Complicates Privatization', *Finance East Europe*, vol. 1, no. 8, 6 November 1991, p. 5. Although the quote in the text concerns the Hungarian situation, that in Poland is not at all different; see, e. g., J. Szperkowicz, 'Samozjady' [Enterprises eating themselves up], *Gazeta Wyborcza*, 25 September 1991, and R. Kubiak, 'Obieg walizkowy: Dyrekcje i zalogi przejadaja zaklad do golych murow' [Money in the Suitcase: Managers and workers eat enterprises up, leaving bare walls], *Wokanda*, 10 November 1991.

18 See various papers by A. Brzeski from the University of California, Davis; most recently, 'Privatising Soviet-type Economies', in *St Petersburg-Leningrad Papers: How to Save the Soviet Economy*, Centre for Research into Communist Economies, London, 1991, and his comments at the Conference on Slovene Privatisation in Bled, 7–9 February 1992.

19 From K. Dervis and T. Condon, 'Hungary: an emerging gradualist success story?' NBER Conference on Transition in Eastern Europe, Cambridge, Mass., 26–29 February 1992.

# 2 Czecho-Slovak survey

*Martin Kupka, Zdenek Tuma and Jozef Zieleniec*

## INTRODUCTION[1]

Looking at the whole spectrum of systems extending between the extremes of pure command and pure market, one could find the Czecho-Slovak economy of the period starting in early 1950s and ending in 1990, undisputably close to the former. Nevertheless, due to a combination of persistence of those few market elements and the pre-war tradition, Czecho-Slovakia pursued relatively sound monetary and fiscal policies, achieving, *inter alia*, a state budget close to balance, low rates of open and hidden inflation, only limited monetary overhang and relatively low foreign indebtedness.

Between 1987 and 1989, net material product (NMP), as measured by official statistics, was growing by just over 2 per cent annually. Private consumption grew in the same period only modestly, the consumer price index (officially measured inflation) increased slightly, external debt in convertible currencies increased by about 10 per cent per annum, and the state budget was slightly in the red throughout the period.

Under Husak's regime the economic reforms were very limited indeed. Thus, Czecho-Slovakia – unlike Hungary and Poland – was beginning the reform from a 'cold start'. None the less, the reform began from a position of comparatively low foreign indebtedness, relative macroeconomic stability, and the existence of basic infrastructure and of longstanding industrial tradition. On the negative, in some spheres of economic transformation (such as the tax reform and the formation of the entrepreneurial class), Czecho-Slovakia still lags behind Hungary and Poland. For the most part, these shortcomings should not affect the design and implementation of the transition programme, but rather the speed with which the programme's success becomes reality.

The 'velvet revolution' took place in November 1989, but an explicitly formulated concept of post-communist reform was not ready until May 1990, mainly because of the difference of opinion within the Czecho-Slovak government. The major impediments to reaching a fast agreement on the reform were differences on the concept and speed of privatization, and the extent of the initial devaluation of the currency that should accompany the introduction of convertibility and liberalization of prices and trade. The rudiments of the programme were later elaborated in the so-called 'Scenario of the Economic Reform', which was then accepted by the Czecho-Slovak parliament. The essential elements of the scenario of the reform have included:

- continuation of macroeconomic austerity plan
- development of the legal framework appropriate for a market economy
- creation of new institutions required for a market economy
- commercialization and privatization of state enterprises
- liberalization of prices and foreign trade
- introduction of limited convertibility of the Czecho-Slovak koruna (the crown).

By 1 January 1991 the key macroeconomic elements of the Czecho-Slovak economic reform had already been put in place: the majority of prices were liberalized, the currency was declared to be 'internally convertible', and the foreign trade liberalized. These policies were complemented by continuation of the macroeconomic austerity. Important external support for the reform was secured through the agreement with the International Monetary Fund, which stipulated for standby credit arrangement totalling $ 1.78 billion, of which $ 833 million were earmarked for facilitation of trade liberalization and currency convertibility. Additionally, on 1 January 1991 the central bank discount rate was raised to 10 per cent, which was also reflected in an increase of the interest rate ceiling on loans at commercial banks from 13 per cent to 24 per cent over the period from mid-November 1990 to early January 1991.

Microeconomic reforms, such as creation of a new legal framework, privatization of state enterprises, and the creation of an adequate safety net continued from 1990. In that area progress has been noticeable, but generally the reform proceeded at a somewhat slower pace than had been initially envisaged by the government when it formulated the reform scenario.

The initial working assumptions of the government as to the economic performance in 1991 were that the state sector's output would decline by 5–10 per cent, upon liberalization, prices would increase rapidly by approximately 30 per cent to stabilize later on, and the velocity of money would increase by some 5 per cent. Monetary and credit targets were expected to partially accommodate the price increases. It should be noted, though, that these targets had been elaborated under the assumption of the exchange rate equal to 24 crowns per US dollar: in reality the exchange rate of 28 crowns per US dollar was adopted. Additionally, a 20 per cent surcharge on imports was introduced.

## THE SECOND HALF OF 1991: TENDENCIES OF THE FIRST HALF CONTINUE

The primary targets of economic policy, i.e. stabilization of the price level and of the Czecho-Slovak crown, remained the same throughout 1991. They were pursued through restrictive monetary and fiscal policies. Economic policy was largely successful in meeting these targets, and stabilizing tendencies observed since the third month of the transition were reinforced in the second half of the year. On the other hand, output fell by an unprecedented 16 per cent.

Without any closer examination the monetary stabilization looks less of a success. When we compare goals announced by the government for 1991 (30 per cent inflation and 5 per cent fall in output) with the actually attained figures (nearly 60 per cent inflation and more than a 16 per cent drop in output), the results must look disappointing. We must see, however, what is behind the figures.

High inflation, as measured by changes in the consumer price index, was due to a large, 25.8 per cent jump in prices in January 1991. It was practically impossible to predict whether the jump would be 10 or 30 per cent. The crucial point was the success or failure of the subsequent stabilization. The consumer price index (table 2.1) indicates that after three months inflation was under control. In the second quarter, inflation was still increasing by around 25 per cent on the annual basis, but from July to October it was practically zero. The end of the year again witnessed a 10–20 per cent inflation. Thus, average inflation reached 57.9 per cent on the annual basis and 53.6 per cent on the December–December basis.

The output tendencies were far less favourable. A GDP decrease of

*Table 2.1*   Month-on-month changes in credit and CPI (in per cent)

|        | Jan  | Feb | Mar | Apr | May | Jun | Jul  | Aug | Sep | Oct  | Nov | Dec |
|--------|------|-----|-----|-----|-----|-----|------|-----|-----|------|-----|-----|
| Credit | -0.3 | 4.3 | 2.0 | 3.4 | 2.2 | 1.9 | 3.2  | 1.3 | 0.6 | 2.1  | 2.5 | 0.9 |
| CPI    | 25.8 | 7.0 | 4.7 | 2.0 | 1.9 | 1.8 | -0.1 | 0.0 | 0.3 | -0.1 | 1.6 | 1.2 |

*Source*: Federal Statistical Office

roughly 16 per cent *vis-à-vis* 1990 was registered in 1991. Industrial production is reported to have fallen by 23 per cent, while construction output by 35 per cent (both in real terms). The fall seems to be extremely severe in the clothing industry (40.4 per cent), textiles (35.6 per cent), non-ferrous metals (41.6 per cent) and electrical engineering (39.2 per cent).

Critics of the transition programme state that the drop has been caused by excessively restrictive policy. Recent estimates[2] show, however, that the exogenous shocks (among them mainly the break-down of the COMECON and the economic collapse of the former Soviet Union), were the most important factors accounting for the fall in output. It is said that 50–75 per cent of the fall was due to these shocks.[3]

External shocks aside, it is difficult to say whether there have been reliable statistical data in this period of abrupt changes. As for the output, for instance, the unreported economic activity may be higher in comparison with recent years, so that the drop in output could be a couple of percentage points lower than reported.

The present authors can hardly believe that a shift to an expansionary policy could lead to a better performance. The crucial point is the ability of the supply side of the economy to adjust, and this has not happened. An across-the-board expansion, either monetary or fiscal, would therefore have a negligible effect on output. The question is whether the authorities could have done more for strengthening the supply side, especially in the private sector: we shall come to this issue later on.

The change in the rate of unemployment lags far behind that of output (i.e. labour productivity is decreasing substantially). In fact, the rate of unemployment at the end of 1991 (6.6 per cent, i.e. 523,700 jobless people), was considerably lower than expected in December 1990. It mainly reflects two developments. First, in spite of the proclamations about radical reform, social policy is very 'soft'. The government did not dare to allow enterprises to go bankrupt. In fact, the whole economy is waiting for large-scale privatization and, in the meantime, there is nobody to control and put pressure on managers of state-owned enterprises. After all, the election is coming, and obviously the government tries its best to avoid any serious social tensions. Furthermore, the government wants the market to decide who will survive. The principal-agent problem has therefore become one of the most serious ones in the Czecho-Slovak economy;[4] we shall be dealing with it in more detail when analysing institutional changes and privatization.

Second, the firms themselves have no internal incentives to go bankrupt or start the layoffs, either. They prefer to reduce working hours or just postpone more serious decisions. The low unemployment rate (relative to the drop in output) is not sustainable in the long run.

The regionally unequal distribution of unemployment has remained a fact. The difference is most striking between the Czech (4.1 per cent) and Slovak (11.8 per cent), but it varies considerably also within each of the two republics. The problem of unemployment is further aggravated by the low mobility of the population, caused not only by habits but also by insufficient housing supply in many regions. It should be stressed that the difference between the levels of unemployment in the Czech Republic and the Slovak Republic is not only a consequence of the less favourable production structure in Slovakia, but also of a more generous unemployment benefits legislation there.

The CSFR data on unemployment when compared to most Western statistics, are biased upwards. It is mainly due to the fact that the inexperienced employment offices are rarely able to differentiate between those actually seeking a job and those already working on the black market or not willing to work at all.

The level of inventories exhibited a strange pattern of change. They were growing sharply till May and since then have begun a gradual decline (see table 2.2). This behaviour was related to a more general tendency: the enterprises realized huge profits at the beginning of 1991 and more or less kept the level of production unchanged. But aggregate demand dropped at the same time by a considerable extent. As already mentioned, the responses of the supply side are slow, if they exist at all: obviously, the enterprises overestimated the demand for their products. Thus, the enterprises were producing for inventories and only later started reducing production.

For several reasons the slowly maturing private sector could not fill the resulting gap in output. First, private business had been banned and – in consequence – forgotten in Czecho-Slovakia for more than 40 years,

*Table 2.2*    Inventories in the Czecho-Slovak economy (in billions of crowns)

| Jan | Feb | Mar | Apr | May | Jun | Jul | Aug | Sep | Oct | Nov | Dec |
|------|------|------|------|-------|------|------|------|------|------|------|------|
| 30.5 | 61.2 | 67.2 | 84.3 | 100.7 | 83.4 | 88.9 | 97.0 | 81.8 | 76.2 | 63.7 | 58.0 |

*Source*: Ministry for Economic Policy and Development of the Czech Republic

and people are often reluctant to leave their regular, until very recently relatively risk-free jobs. Second, during 1991 the newly opened small businesses got from the state and financial institutions virtually the same treatment as big state companies. This implies that it was rather difficult for them to gather the necessary capital and to expand.

The quickly growing number of official permissions to start private businesses is a misleading indicator of the private business expansion (over 1.3 million were issued by December 1991), as many of these 'businessmen' do it only as a part-time job or do not even do it at all. Moreover, most private firms used the so-called 'Schwarz system', which means that they hired other private firms, consisting of one employee, to do business for them on a subcontract basis. In other words, one firm, let us say with 50 workers, hired effectively 50 private agents. The system was very efficient for tax evasion purposes because firms did not have to pay the payroll tax or the social insurance contributions. But the Schwarz system was forbidden at the end of 1991 and we expect that the number of 'businessmen' will consequently decline.

Another implemented change is that the applicant for a registration (permission) must now pay kcs 3,000, which is 30 times more than two years ago. This fee will probably contribute to a decrease in the number of future applicants.

The most important reason for unsatisfactory development in the private sector was the approach of the government. Its efforts in supporting small businesses were negligible, and only in the last quarter of 1991 did the situation change. The department that develops a strategy of support for small businesses has been established at the Federal Ministry of Economy. Also, in 1992 Českomoravskà zàručni a rozvojovà banka (The Czech-Moravian Bank for Securities and Development) came into operation.[5] This bank is supposed to provide collateral for loans at commercial banks, subsidize interest rate, and perform other services for the small business sector.

Collateral requirements for loans, as everywhere in East Central Europe, made access to credit difficult for private businessmen; and commercial banks did not always understand what collateral was.[6] They required the same type of collateral from state enterprises and from the private sector, usually fully covering the value of the loan. But it is obvious that there is a fundamental difference between collateral of the state firm, which has state property at its disposal and collateral in the form of, say, a businessman's house. This behaviour of commercial banks placed the private sector at a disadvantage, especially in the case of long-term loans. In spite of this, in the second half of the year credits to the private sector showed more dynamics (they had greater absolute increments) than those given to state enterprises (see table 2.3).

*Table 2.3* Credits to the non-private and private sector, 1991 (billions of crowns)

|  | *Dec/90* | *Mar* | *Jun* | *Sep* | *Dec* |
|---|---|---|---|---|---|
| non-private | 532.6 | 558.4 | 586.6 | 602.0 | 611.0 |
| private | 3.4 | 9.4 | 24.7 | 40.6 | 63.0 |

*Source*: National Bank of Czecho-Slovakia

## MONETARY AND FISCAL POLICIES

Monetary and fiscal policies were the backbone of the economic transition in 1991. They were to stop inflation and succeeded in doing so. The prescription for a restrictive fiscal policy is quite clear: reduce subsidies and keep the government expenditure under control. But what should one try to achieve with monetary policy, what kind of 'anchors' should be applied during transition?

Theory suggests[7] that the effect of demand shocks can be alleviated by indexation. But it also says that indexation does not work in the case of supply shocks. And the Czecho-Slovak economy has suffered from both shocks. At the end of 1990, the aggregate demand went up because the increasing uncertainty with respect to prospective price level changed expectations and the households tried to transform savings into consumer goods (and other usual hedges against inflation). As mentioned above, the economy was also hit by supply shocks, and under those conditions any theory-based concept of economic policy was error-prone. Targeting money supply was difficult because money demand was unpredictable, and targeting exchange rates could have induced strong pressures on reserves.

The central bank (National Bank of Czecho-Slovakia) applied both targets, using in addition tools such as ceilings on credits and interest rates. In January 1991 money supply was restricted, inducing a credit crunch. Afterwards, the squeeze was relaxed and after stabilization of the price level in April 1991, the growth of credit became positive in real terms (see table 2.1). In spite of this fact, enterprises encountered severe payment difficulties and insolvency became a serious problem across the whole economy. A decision was taken to issue bonds worth kcs 50 billion, which would supersede some of SOEs bad debts *vis-à-vis* commercial banks, and to improve the level of capitalization of commercial banks.

The bonds were floated by the National Property Funds.[8] The bonds became assets in the balance sheet of commercial banks, and in exchange for this banks wrote off loans (or a part of them) of evaluated enterprises. Later, the bonds will be exchanged for shares of privatized enterprises, i.e. for those shares which the state will have kept. Though kcs 50 billion (or kcs 40 billion, see below) represented only a part of the total sum of SOEs' debt, it has been expected to help in making the financial system work again, as well as to be able to influence the economy through monetary policy. For the time being, even if enterprises are financially squeezed, they continue to do business.

The bond issue in question pursued simultaneously another aim – to improve the capital adequacy ratio of the banks. It ranged from 1.5 to 4 per cent, whereas the requirement for newly founded banks is 8 per cent. Therefore, kcs 10 billion out of the total was devoted to this purpose so that banks which were still state-owned would reach a capital adequacy ratio of at least 5 per cent.

An important anchor of economic policy was the exchange rate. After three devaluations in 1990, the official and the parallel exchange rates nearly met. High demand for foreign currency at the beginning of the year, caused by the price effect of successive devaluations and flight from the crown by the general public, were gradually disappearing. Excess demand was dampened by limits set on foreign currency purchases by individuals, import surcharges,[9] and by payment rules applied for imports. As soon as the shock from liberalization was absorbed by the economy, demand matched supply and the exchange rate became stable even without considerable intervention by the Central Bank. Thus, one source of disequilibria – the distorted exchange rates – has disappeared. On the other hand, the Marshall-Lerner condition has been obviously violated in Czechoslovakia in the short run, so that the liberalization of foreign trade, together with the devaluation, must have contributed to inflation.[10] On balance, however, the developments on the foreign exchange market are, and must be considered advantageous. After initial interventions by the Central Bank, the crown remained stable and the official exchange rate approached that of the informal market. The interventions by the Central Bank were over time less and less needed, which resulted in an increase in the Central Bank's reserves. After all, nobody should expect the exchange rate to approach purchasing power parity. Parallel exchange rate was an obvious target in the first phase of external liberalization. Gradual revaluations will emerge only along with the improving export performance in the tradeable goods' sector.

The evaluation of monetary and fiscal policies cannot be reduced to their 'technical' aspects. Economic policy is a game: a game resting on expectations. This is especially true for the transition period. Firm commitments represented by simple monetary and budgetary rules are sought after. Any diversion from a commitment would have adverse impact on agents' behaviour. Thus, even if we could find 'technically' optimal policies, they might be strongly time-inconsistent. Therefore, the present authors see the 1991 monetary policy as an important pillar of stabilization, though we could raise some objections, such as the excessively severe squeeze in January, or the needlessly late attempt to solve the threatening insolvency of industrial SOEs.

In parallel with monetary policy, fiscal stance was also planned to be restrictive. Together with the former policy, it was planned to reduce inflationary pressures and enhance credibility. Further, by reducing the share of budgetary expenditures in GDP, *inter alia* by removing subsidies, it aimed at creating an environment without price distortions.

The proposed budget for 1991 envisaged a year-end surplus totalling to kcs 8 billion. But the actual pattern of the budget balance was surprisingly different. The year started with a huge surplus reaching in May a peak of about kcs 21 billion and ended with a deficit of half that size (see table 2.4). Let us have a closer look at the second half, and mainly at the end of 1991.

The unexpectedly large surplus in the mid-year enabled the government to provide some extra money to the neediest sectors, such as health care and education. Hospitals, universities, etc. did not manage to spend the money immediately, so that their spending lagged behind appropriations until, by and large, the last two months of 1991. At the beginning of February 1992, the total deficit for 1991 amounted to kcs

*Table 2.4*   Total budget surplus aggregate budgetary stance in 1991 (minus sign signifies a deficit; in billions of crowns)

| Jan | Feb | Mar | Apr | May | Jun | Jul | Aug | Sep | Oct | Nov | Dec |
|-----|-----|-----|-----|-----|-----|-----|-----|-----|-----|-----|-----|
| 1.4 | 6.9 | 15.3 | 16.3 | 20.9 | 17.7 | 13.0 | 9.9 | 11.4 | 8.0 | −2.7 | −12.3 |

*Source*: Pokladni plněni stàtniho rozpočtu (Data on implementation of the state budget)

17 billion, to which the Czech republic contributed 13.3 and the Slovak republic kcs 8.9 billion, while the federal budget was in surplus of kcs 5.2 billion. Some bills came later, so the final deficit was kcs 12.3 billion. These expenditures were in some cases a waste of money, but fortunately they did not change radically the stance of fiscal policy over the year as a whole. In general, fiscal policy did work restrictively, and billions wasted in December could not overturn its overall stabilizing effect. It is, however, an indication of threats hanging over 1992.

As to the structure of the budget, the major change concerned the decentralization of expenditures. Now the republics themselves decide on far larger shares of spending. But besides this, nothing of substance happened in the public finance. The revenue structure has remained the same: there are still three pillars upon which revenues rest, namely: profit tax on SOEs, payroll tax and turnover tax. The expenditure side is a bit more interesting. The governmental policy aimed at substantially reducing the budget, mainly through cutting down the subsidies. It has really happened, but there was an exception. The government has removed practically all retail trade subsidies (negative turnover tax on some consumer goods) and subsidies in foreign trade, but subsidies to enterprises slightly increased, though in nominal terms only. This reflects a cautious approach to SOEs on the side of the government. In fact, the government is waiting for privatization to take place and expects that the market will deliver the verdict on who is going to become bankrupt.

The budget still represents over 60 per cent of NMP (according to the old formula) and major changes will presumably come about only in 1993 – along with the planned tax reform.

The Czecho-Slovak foreign trade developed in 1991 relatively satisfactorily. Without doubt, the determining factor was the breakdown of the old COMECON markets, which forced enterprises' managers to look for new outlets westwards. Their efforts were supported by a considerable devaluation of the local currency which took place in December 1990. Its magnitude, looked at in retrospect, proved to be quite correct. Exchange rate did not have to be adjusted during the year. Nor did it cause any strong pressure on foreign currency reserves within the same time span. There was also another stimulus for domestic producers to export, i.e. the weakened domestic demand resulting from the continuing decline in real incomes.

In spite of the lip-service often paid by many Western politicians to free trade in general and to opening up their economies to the transforming economies of East Central Europe in particular, the availability of the EC markets remained fairly limited to our producers. At one point, France even initiated postponement of the ratification of the association agreement between the CSFR and the EC, due to fears of possible Czecho-Slovak exports of agricultural products. Faced with the stubborn protectionism of developed economies with respect to imports, Czecho-Slovak diplomacy attempted to find another way to expand export of domestic products in exchange for convertible currency earnings. The 'triangular plan' entailed exporting to the former Soviet Union, with the exported goods paid for by Western aid funds directly to Czecho-Slovak producers. The plan was basically approved. It remains to be seen, however, how much of their own potential exports Western countries are going to sacrifice on this account.

After the devaluation imports became expensive, but as domestic inflation continued, the gap between the prices of domestic and imported goods began to close. Under the regime of limited internal convertibility of domestic currency, trade with imported goods flourished, to the frustration of domestic producers who complained of insufficient state protection. It is true that low tariffs and absence of import duties on the one hand, coupled with heavy taxation of domestic producers, on the other, led sometimes to inequitable treatment of domestic and foreign competitors. This became most apparent in the car market. In reaction to complaints of Czecho-Slovak enterprises, import restrictions, which were loosened after January 1991, were partially reintroduced in the second half of the year. Among other measures, the tariff schedule was reconstructed, which reflected a new active role to be played by tariffs in an economy without state monopoly of foreign trade. The new tariff schedule initially met with the disapproval of trading partners who were upset by the fact that the average level of protection moved up slightly. Czecho-Slovakia still has the lowest average protection level in East Central Europe and one of the lowest in the world.

After several decades of Soviet dominance, Germany became the most important foreign trade partner of Czecho-Slovakia. The total value of Czecho-Slovak exports in 1991 amounted to kcs 321.2 billion, the total value of imports was kcs 293.7 billion (both in f.o.b. prices). Hence, there is a balance of trade surplus of kcs 27.5 billion. As to the commodity structure of foreign trade, there have been few important changes. The most remarkable seems to be the political pressure for rapid reduction of arms exports and the increasing role of the tourist industry as a foreign exchange earner.

Foreign investment is considered to be an important way of increasing the volume of fixed capital and of improving a country's economic performance. There often are important by-products accompanying the employment of capital originating in the West: know-how, marketing skills, inflow of advanced technology and new opportunities for exports. From the point of view of capital inflows, however, 1991 was not a successful year – at least when compared to, for instance, Hungarian achievements. In 1991 the total value of direct foreign investments in Czecho-Slovakia amounted to only about kcs 1 billion. The reason was not, as often maintained, the obsolete infrastructure, which in Hungary is hardly any better, nor some hypothetical disadvantageous conditions for establishing foreign enterprises, but, as many investors put it openly, the unclear political future, most importantly with respect to continuing nationalist quarrels.

There is a remarkable difference between the amount of foreign capital coming to the Czech Republic and to the Slovak Republic. One reason is that Slovakia cannot offer a long record of industrial tradition. The labour force is less disciplined and less achievement-oriented there, and the potential political risk stemming from the considerable popularity of nationalist and socialist political parties is higher. It is generally expected that after the June 1992 elections – if the outcome of the elections is seen as reassuring *vis-à-vis* further continuation of reforms – the capital inflow into Czecho-Slovakia will gain momentum. Other important factors facilitating the expansion of foreign investors into the country in the near future will be the growing weight of the private sector due to continuing privatization as well as the commencement of operation of the capital markets which will also make possible the portfolio foreign investment. It is obvious that the more successful the whole transformation is, *ceteris paribus*, the less risky will foreign investors regard their prospective operations.

As far as the structure of foreign investment is concerned, the same problems which occurred in the first half of 1991 continue to persist. Only a few relatively large investment contracts have been signed, while most of the remaining contracts are, by Western standards, rather modest in size. Even if the investment project is reported to be large, it will often be spread over a considerable period and/or financed in other than cash form. The bulk of foreign investment has come from Germany and Austria. The South-east Asian 'Little Dragons' and Japan seem to have had little interest.

The economic nationalism of the population arising out of fears of selling national wealth at bargain-basement prices has weakened over 1991, in spite of the fact that such fears have been occasionally revived by rather unfortunate declarations and demands by foreign, mostly German investors, who requested highly preferential treatment, coupled with protection against external competition. Nonetheless German firms may be more successful in competition with other firms, because they have better knowledge of the Czecho-Slovak cultural and economic environment. If Czecho-Slovakia wants to diversify its trade and investment ties, it will have to provide better information abroad. Germany and Austria may obtain information easily but the Czecho-Slovak government should be more active with respect to potential overseas investors.

## INSTITUTIONAL CHANGES

Privatization is the most important pillar of the transformation programme at the microlevel. It is the *sine qua non* without which the economic reform would be doomed to failure. It is also the priority of governmental economic policy for 1992, after having shifted away from macroeconomic equilibrium priorities in 1991, since without it any substantial shift of the aggregate supply curve rightward can hardly occur.

The programme of small-scale privatization launched in January 1991 continued throughout the year at the pace shown in table 2.5. In October, an amendment to the law on small-scale privatization was passed by the parliament, reflecting the need to correct some imperfections of the law revealed by experience. The amendment extended the minimum time length of a rent contract between the auction winner and the restituted owner of the land, upon which the operational unit is located, in order to strengthen the winner's incentive to invest in the unit. Second, the amendment forbids the so-called Dutch auction in the first round if landed property is a part of the operational unit to be auctioned. Third, to make the operations of both domestic and foreign law-evaders more difficult, the amendment introduced severe financial penalties for auction winners who refuse to actually implement purchase of the operational unit they won. The operational unit in question would be later auctioned under the same conditions as if it had never been auctioned before.

*Table 2.5*   Small-scale privatization in 1991: cumulative number and value of auctioned units

|        | Mar | Jun  | Jul   | Aug   | Sep   | Oct   | Nov   | Dec   |
|--------|-----|------|-------|-------|-------|-------|-------|-------|
| number | 712 | 7475 | 10108 | 12299 | 14775 | 17079 | 19638 | 19774 |
| value[a] | 302 | 4142 | 6143  | 8209  | 11668 | 16001 | 20938 | 23272 |

*Note*:[a]cumulative, in millions
*Source*: Ministry for Economic Policy and Development of the Czech Republic

The process of small-scale privatization would have evolved quicker in the last two months of 1991 if a new decree on real estate pricing had not driven initial asking prices dramatically up. Another break for small-scale privatization was the rapidly approaching large-scale privatization, which energizes the management of state enterprises, giving them the chance to retain control over their respective operational units by including them into privatization projects.

The legislative discrimination against foreigners who are legally excluded from the first round of auctions (in order to improve the odds of relatively financially weaker domestic small and medium-scale entrepreneurs), found its unexpected international echo in the last days of 1991, when an important state agreement on restoring friendly relations with Germany was prepared.

The Sudeten Germans, expelled from Czecho-Slovakia after World War II, protested against the prepared wording that did not mention their property claims, but on the contrary, confirmed *de facto* their expropriation by not admitting them to participate in the first round of auctions (the fact that all foreigners have been excluded was obviously of little importance for the Germans in question). The ratification of the agreement was postponed by several weeks, but it took place none-theless.

The process of restitution continued in parallel with the small-scale privatization, but was less emotional, less burdened with such phenomena as suspected laundering of 'dirty' money, collusion, cheating, speculation and occasional acts of violence. From the point of view of consumers, restitutions are often more welcome, as the new owners mostly do not try to maximize profits as much as possible from the acquired property in the shortest possible time and do not change the product composition so profoundly. The institutions responsible for the restitution have worked smoothly so far, and it seems that the fears of those opposing the restitution at the beginning of the transition were not fully justified. On the other hand, it is true that restitutions sometimes put an effective break on privatization postponing the decision on who the real owner is till an uncertain date in the future.

More important for the transition to the desired private property dominance is the large-scale privatization that started in the autumn of 1991. Unlike the small-scale one, large-scale privatization is not restricted either to the chosen form of privatization (outright sale to selected buyers, auctions, sealed-bid tenders, sale of shares on capital markets, etc.) or to the nationality of buyers. Large-scale privatization is scheduled to be realized in several waves, with the first two waves expected to be completed by the end of 1992. It is estimated that through the large-scale privatization the state is going to get rid of about 85 per cent of its industrial property.

The government, in fact the Federal and Republic governments, decide in which wave a given enterprise is to be privatized. Privatization of each enterprise is based on a privatization project prepared according to the rules specifying the procedure by the management of the concerned firm. The project has to cover the whole enterprise. Besides the basic privatization project designed by the management, there are also competing privatization projects considered by responsible ministries that may be prepared by virtually anybody interested, even if they deal with the privatization of only a part of the whole enterprise. The final form of privatization of each enterprise is determined by the respective ministry charged with privatization.

Before being privatized, most state enterprises are converted into joint-stock companies owned by the state that – after having the privatization project approved – become part of the National Property Funds, which are responsible for the completion of their privatization according to the project's specification. Three per cent of equity in each privatized joint-stock company is reserved by law for the purpose of restitution. There has been some pressure to include a considerable portion of the remaining shares into voucher privatization.

Voucher privatization has developed rather dramatically in Czecho-Slovakia. Since 1 November 1991, voucher booklets and 1000 kcs stamps have been sold at all post offices. The state promised to deliver shares in accounting value of about 210 billion kcs on the supply side. It was expected that there would be about 4 million participants (out of 11.5 millions eligible) in the first wave of voucher privatization. The registration of so called investment coupon holders (DIKs in Czech) opened on 1 December and was scheduled to last until the end of January.

At the end of 1991 the whole programme looked as if it were to be a fiasco. The demand side, i.e. the number of registered people, was rather low. The main reason for that was probably a badly designed advertising campaign. The attitude of ordinary people towards voucher privatization changed only after an investment privatization fund[11] offered to those who would entrust their investment coupon booklets to them to pay kcs 10,000 after a year if they wanted to sell their shares. By the end of January 1992 there were more than 8 million DIKs in Czecho-Slovakia, largely locating their investment coupon booklets in more than 400 approved state-owned and privately-owned investment funds. There have also been some questions raised aimed at the responsible officials. Among questions asked, three made the headlines: How to increase the volume of property offered? How to ensure that all people willing to participate can register? How to limit in advance the looming financial and economic power of large investment funds?

The third problem, paradoxically enough, is the reverse of an objection often raised earlier in 1991 by critics of voucher privatization, which was the objection to overly dispersed ownership. In contrast, it is the concentration of shares in a few investment funds that became largely feared.

It is difficult to say today how justified those worries are because the related legislation has not been completed yet. It would be dangerous, however, for the credibility of the government to change abruptly and on an *ad hoc* basis either the explicit rules or the implicit philosophy of voucher privatization. It would be even more dangerous, considering that the people might be already a bit nervous about some technical imperfections which have led to the postponement of the actual start of the first wave of voucher privatization by a couple of weeks.

## CONCLUSIONS AND PERSPECTIVES

The year 1991 in Czecho-Slovakia can be seen as successful: the economy has survived the beginning of the transition (see table 2.6). Restrictive monetary and fiscal policies were the stepping stones of the struggle to get post-liberalization inflation under control and establish macroeconomic equilibrium. In spite of some reservations with respect to inter-enterprise credit undermining the effectiveness of tight monetary policy, or the year-end budget deficit, the policy course has been maintained. But the problems mentioned above indicate that 1992 may decide whether Czecho-Slovakia will follow the Polish path of quickly increasing problems in the industrial and budget-financed sectors.

For the majority of the public and presumably also for the government[12] at the federal and republican levels, the priority for 1992 is thought to be privatization. But the present authors see as equally important the budget balance. The collapse of the budgetary discipline would be for the transition as large a blow (in the short run at least) as a failure of privatization. The budget for 1992 is very taut, and in our opinion it will hardly be possible to maintain it even roughly in balance, as it is hoped by the Federal government. A fall in output, if it continues, will reduce revenues and, at the same time, a strong pressure is expected on the expenditure side.

And we do expect output to go further down by 7–8 per cent, the unemployment rate to exceed 10 per cent, and inflation to approach 15 per cent. These estimates must be seen as optimistic, depending crucially on the promising internal political developments and a stimulating external economic environment. With respect to the coming election, one should consider at least two scenarios: one for Czech countries and Slovakia, the second for Czecho-Slovakia. Even if nationalism in Slovakia is not sufficiently strong to start on a path leading to independence – which is probable – the Federal parliament will likely be too fragmented to be a workable body. Thus, economic forecasts for 1992 may be formulated only under the condition of 'political things being equal'.[13]

*Table 2.6*    General data on Czecho-Slovak economy

|  | 1988 | 1989 | 1990 | 1 | 2 | 3 | 4 | 1991 |
|---|---|---|---|---|---|---|---|---|
| NMP, nom. | 606.4 | 618.1 | 673.2 | 214.1 | 200.3 | 188.5 | 218.6 | 821.5 |
| NMP, real |  | 576.3 | 570.1 | 122.4 | 115.6 | 102.6 | 115.0 | 455.6 |
| Δ NMP, real | n.a. | n.a. | −1.1 | −7.4 | −19.3 | −25.8 | −26.5 | −20.1 |
| GDP, real | n.a. | n.a. | 727.0 | 163.6 | 157.1 | 138.9 | 148.0 | 607.6 |
| Δ GDP, real |  |  | −5.1 | −14.1 | −22.1 | −23.6 | −16.4 |
| Indstr. pr., Δ | 2.1 | 1.1 | −3.7 | −9.3 | −20.9 | −29.2 | −33.0 | −23.1 |
| Constr., Δ | 0.1 | 1.7 | −6.6 | −28.9 | −34.4 | −31.7 | −28.6 | −30.9 |
| Inventories |  |  | 594.4 | 637.2 | 658.7 | 662.5 | 615.9 | 615.9 |
| Emplmnt, total | 0.5 | −0.1 | −3.5 | −8.9 | −11.9 | −15.0 | −16.9 | −12.5 |
| Empl., indstr. | 0.5 | 0.0 | −3.4 | −8.5 | −11.3 | −14.2 | −15.2 | −12.3 |
| Unempl., abs. | − | 0.1 | 77.0 | 184.6 | 300.8 | 446.2 | 523.7 | 523.7 |
| Unempl., rate | − | 0.0 | 1.0 | 2.3 | 3.8 | 5.6 | 6.6 | 6.6 |
| Private firms[a] | 51.1 | 86.8 | 488.4 | 655.0 | 921.0 | 1131.0 | 1338.4 | 1338.4 |
| CPI | 0.2 | 1.4 | 10.0 | 54.7 | 68.5 | 56.3 | 52.7 | 57.9 |
| PPI |  | −0.7 | 4.5 | 66.6 | 69.7 | 72.1 | 69.9 | 69.9 |
| Wage, month av.[b] | 3054 | 3123 | 3238 | 3314 | 3592 | 3672 | 4522 | 3775 |
| Wage, real,Δ[b] | 2.0 | 0.8 | −5.8 | −30.2 | −26.8 | −23.8 | −14.6 | −24.3 |
| Income, nom.Δ[c] | 4.2 | 3.5 | 7.4 | 7.2 | 13.1 | 12.2 | 13.1 | 13.1 |
| DD+TD+FCD[d] |  | 279.4 | 280.5 | 282.5 | 290.2 | 300.0 | 331.6 | 331.6 |
| FCD, hshlds | 0.9 | 1.7 | 9.8 | 13.5 | 18.1 | 22.4 | 26.6 | 26.6 |
| M1 | 309.5 | 311.1 | 291.2 | 279.9 | 294.3 | 324.7 | 347.1 | 347.1 |
| M2 | 529.4 | 547.8 | 550.7 | 545.7 | 583.9 | 626.1 | 672.2 | 672.2 |
| Crdit, enterpr. | − | 530.8 | 536.0 | 567.8 | 611.3 | 642.6 | 646.1[e] | 646.1[e] |
| Crdit, private |  | 3.4 | 9.4 | 24.7 | 40.6 | 63.0 | 63.0 |
| Discount |  | 5.6 | 10.0 | 10.0 | 9.5 | 9.5 | 9.5 |
| Intrst, avrg[f] |  | 14.68 | 15.14 | 14.20 | 13.94 | 14.46 |
| Budget-revn. | 404.0 | 415.4 | 463.5 | 108.8 | 222.2 | 350.0 | 466.2 |
| Budget-exp. | 401.2 | 415.0 | 455.9 | 93.5 | 204.5 | 338.6 | 484.8 |
| Budget-srpls | +2.8 | +0.4 | +7.6 | 15.3 | 17.7 | 11.4 | −18.6 | −12.3[g] |
| Subsidies | 96.1 | 122.1 | 105.9 | 12.8 | 14.9 | 20.7 | 19.8 | 68.2 |
| ER, kcs/$, offc[h] | 14.36 | 15.05 | 17.39 | 27.88 | 30.32 | 30.52 | 29.20 | 29.48 |
| ER, kcs/$, blck | 33.44 | 42.39 | 39–40 | 34.08 | 31.74 | 32.51 | 30.82 | 32.28 |
| Exports, total[i] | 218.9 | 217.5 | 215.3 | 51.7 | 85.9 | 84.0 | 99.5 | 321.2 |
| – convert. | 76.8 | 87.5 | 114.5 | 44.2 | 79.0 | 79.6 | 96.7 | 299.1 |
| Imports, total | 214.3 | 214.7 | 238.2 | 63.2 | 84.4 | 63.9 | 82.2 | 292.7 |
| – convert. | 78.5 | 83.0 | 127.2 | 58.3 | 80.1 | 61.6 | 80.7 | 280.7 |
| Trade blnce | 4.5 | 2.8 | −22.9 | −11.5 | 1.5 | 20.1 | 17.3 | 27.5 |
| Exprt, Δ, total | 3.9 | −0.6 | −1.0 | −33.7 | −7.2 | −1.3 | 1.5 | 49.2* |
| – west | 15.5 | 13.6 | 28.9 | −12.9 | −8.8 | +13.8 | 65.9 | 161.5* |
| Imprt, Δ, total | 0.7 | 0.2 | 10.9 | −19.7 | −13.6 | −36.3 | −28.3 | +23.3* |
| – west | 14.0 | 6.1 | 43.8 | −18.3 | −18.8 | −24.0 | +8.5 | +120.7* |
| Current acc. |  |  | −1104 | −472.8 | −340.4 | −205.0 | 112.3[g] | 112.3 |
| Indebted., $ | 7281 | 7915 | 8075 | 8261 | 8793 | 9278 | 9285[a] | 9285 |
| Retail, nom., Δ[j] | 4.9 | 3.7 | 11.9 | 10.4 | 3.9 | 0.2 | −3.3 | −3.3 |
| Retail, real, Δ[j] |  |  | −37.1 | −38.0 | −39.6 | −39.9 | −39.9 |

*Notes to Table 2.6:*

[a]private firms: number of issued permissions to perform private economic activities
[b]firms with 100 workers and more
[c]values against the same period in the previous year
[d]DD + TD + FCD: demand deposits + time dep. + foreign currency dep.; all refer to households only
[e]including the removal of bad debts
[f]Intrst, avrg: average interest rate of total credits
[g]revised figure (March) including also local budgets which improved the total by more than kcs 6 bn
[h]official exchange rate, 1991 is not fully comparable with the previous years. It is the average referring to middle values
[i]export, import – millions of US $
[j]retail: both nominal and real – private businesses and firms with less than 100 employees are included by estimate

## NOTES

1  The introduction largely draws on J. Charap, K. Dyba, M. Kupka, 'The reform process in Czechoslovakia: an assessment of recent developments and prospects for the future', *Communist Economies and Economic Transformation*, vol. 4, no. 1, 1992.

2  I. Šujan, 'Rok 1991 a perspektiva 1991 očami statistiky', *Ekonom*, no. 4, 1992.

3  In Finland, which also had large exports to the USSR, the export shortfall is declared to be one of the prime causes of GDP decline in 1991, amounting to about 5 per cent.

4  D. Begg, 'Economic reform in Czechoslovakia: should we believe in Santa Klaus?', *Economic Policy*, 13, October 1991.

5  A similar institution has been founded in Slovakia.

6  W. Charemza, 'Alternative paths to macroeconomic stability in Czechoslovakia', *European Economy*, 1991, special edn. no. 2.

7  It follows from the debate on rules vs. discretion, see also Begg, 'Economic reform in Czechoslovakia'.

8  National Property Funds are established at the level of the republics; these bodies gather the shares of enterprises going to privatization.

9  At the beginning of the year it was 20 per cent, now it is 10 per cent.

10  If prices were liberalized later, the overshooting of exchange rates and prices would be even greater. For a detailed discussion of trade-off between inflation and exchange rates, see Charemza, 'Alternative paths to macroeconomic stability'.

11  An institution collecting and investing points from risk-averse citizens, who in turn receive shares in the fund instead of shares in privatized enterprises. These funds are open-ended but closed for the time being.

12  We are not sure about the priorities of the Slovak government, especially of any future Slovak government.

13  See also A. Bulíř, *Úroková sazba a rovnováha na úverovém trhu*, SBČs, 1992; reports and data from State Czechoslovak Bank, Federal Ministry of Finance, Federal Statistical Office; Z. Tuma, *Monetary and Fiscal Policies in Czechoslovakia during Transition*, Reform Round Table, International Center for Economic Growth, January 1992.

# 3 Hungarian survey

*Mihaly Laki*

In this chapter we shall analyse macroeconomic processes of the period between the first quarter of 1990 and the last months of 1991. The target is to describe the transition process from a centrally planned to a market economy. The structure of the survey starts with a brief description of political and social conditions influencing the Hungarian economy. Thereafter, looking at the main economic indicators, we shall evaluate the performance of the Hungarian economy and the effectiveness of the governmental policies. At the end of the survey we shall evaluate indicators measuring the extent and speed of the transition process. We shall focus on processes which took place in 1991 (with special emphasis on the latter part of the year).

## POLITICS: CONSOLIDATION AND APATHY

It was 1989 that saw the collapse of socialism, while 1990 was a year of radical changes in political institutions. In turn, 1991 can be described as a year of gradual, though only partial, political consolidation.

Looking at the international aspects, 1991 was the year of the withdrawal of Soviet troops from Hungarian soil: a fact of almost symbolic significance. It was also a year of continuing reorientation of the country's international contacts; Hungary became an associated member of the Common Market. Another remarkable factor of the political and economic consolidation was the signing of the three-year agreement between Hungary and the IMF. These actions partly offset the effects of political destabilization of the region (collapse of the Soviet Empire, civil war in Yugoslavia and ethnic conflicts in Romania and Czecho-Slovakia). But the increasing number of legal and illegal immigrants and refugees makes it clear for the Hungarian public that it is impossible to isolate their country and its fragile stability from the region's conflicts and tensions.

In 1989–90, the population itself – or at least a good part of it – played an important, direct role in the political process (see table 3.1). In 1990, it was the parliament, and even more the government, which became the dominant player on the political scene. The time of elections, mass demonstrations, and revolts is over. The main battle-field is the parliament, and the war is over the legislation process. The order of presenting them and, of course, the content of the laws, are in the centre of debates between the opposition and the governing parties.

*Table 3.1*    The share of voters[a] in the eligible population (in per cent)

|  | per cent |
|---|---|
| Referendum (November 1989) | 54.9 |
| General election (April 1990) | 65.1 |
| Referendum (July 1990) | 14.0 |
| Local election | |
| first round (Sept. 1990) | 40.2 |
| second round (Oct. 1990) | 28.9 |
| Public opinion polls: the share of people who are sure that they would participate in the general election | |
| May 1991 | 49.0 |
| October 1991 | 39.0 |
| December 1991 | 40.0 |

*Note:* [a]Unless otherwise indicated

Concerning the economy, the Hungarian parliament passed new laws on the central bank and on monetary institutions. New regulations on concessions, accountancy, and bankruptcy were introduced, as well.

If we look at the timetable of the governmental economic pro-gramme, we will see some delays in the legislation process. (The government – due to political reasons – gave preference to the law on restitution of property to private owners and churches.) Laws con-cerning the reform of the state budget and of the social security system are only in their preparatory stage. A general law on privatization is missing, as well. But all things considered, the development of basic institutions of the market economy takes place at a good pace.

The impressive legislative performance was possible only because of the aforementioned dominance of the parliament and the government over the whole of political life. The population itself has grown – by contrast – extremely passive.

Since the beginning of transition, a considerable part of the population has stood aside from political life. The share of non-voters has been relatively high in this period. This indicator of the political indifference grew further in 1991. Public opinion polls showed at the end of the year that an increasing majority of voters would not take part in the general election. The extremely low share of voters in local and parliamentary by-elections (23–26 per cent) indicates that this is not to be considered only the temporary political behaviour of millions of Hungarians.

Another signal of the political indifference was that the membership of the competing trade union confederations diminished in 1991. Not only the numbers decreased, but the members' passivity weakened the position of the unions. Unsuccessful local and general strikes demonstrated the limited bargaining power of the unions.

This political vacuum strengthened the position of the state bureaucracy, but that of the extremist political forces, as well. The prospects for the antidemocratic forces largely depend on the performance of the economy.

## DETERMINANTS OF MACROECONOMIC DEVELOPMENTS

In 1990 the collapse of the COMECON trade was the most important short term challenge to the Hungarian economy. The sales of Hungarian firms in rouble-calculated trade amounted to 230 billion forints in 1989 and only to 160 billion in 1990. This decline continued in 1991. Exports to the East European countries (former members of the COMECON), except Germany, were 122.6 billion forints (January – November 1991). This is 85.9 per cent of exports in the same period of the previous year. The estimates for December are 11 billion forints, which is a bit more than the year's monthly average. This means that the sales of Hungarian firms to this market may drop to 130–132 billion forints in 1991. The 20 per cent fall in 1991 was smaller than the 30 per cent decrease of the rouble export in 1990. The downfall was also slower in the second half of 1991, than in the first (16–17 per cent and 21–22 per cent, respectively).

There have also been changes in the dynamics of Hungarian imports from the East European countries. In 1990, imports from the post-COMECON countries fell by 11 per cent. In the first quarter of 1991 the volume of those imports was only 78 per cent of the first quarter of the previous year. But in the second quarter, and especially in the second half of the year, these imports (measured in forints) have increased. In the period of January–November imports from Eastern Europe were 28.9 per cent higher than in the same period of 1990. (There is about a 40 per cent deterioration in terms of trade with the post-COMECON countries, therefore there is only insignificant growth or even stagnation in these imports when measured in real terms. But we have to recognize that after a long period characterized by a downward tendency the trend has been reversed.)

There were no beneficial changes on the domestic market in 1991. Retail trade (measured in real terms) fell by 10 per cent in 1990. This tendency continued in 1991, as well. The retail trade in the January–September period fell by 24.3 per cent, compared to the same period of 1990. There are no available data on the extent of the illegal trade. Probably, the share of this trade is growing but it cannot counterbalance the decrease of the legal retail trade.

Not only consumption but also investment expenditures of the population fell in 1991. The number of houses or apartment buildings whose erection started in the first half of 1991 was 67 per cent (!) smaller than in the corresponding period of the previous year.

We have observed a 7.2 per cent decrease of the total investment in 1990, as well (earlier forecast was 9 per cent drop). There was no upturn on this market, either. Taking a cautious estimate, the volume of investment fell by 10 per cent in 1991.

Not only the shrinking demand, but also the phenomenon of so-called 'chains of insolvency' (interfirm involuntary credit resulting from unpaid bills for goods and services) became more of a problem in 1991.

As we may see from table 3.2 the number of (mainly state-owned) firms on the prohibitory list of the Hungarian National Bank grew rapidly and the involuntary credit generated by them was about 1.5 times more in September 1991 than a year before. Involuntary crediting:

- causes cash flow problems of many efficient firms
- makes it impossible to distinguish between permanently and temporarily insolvent firms
- has adverse effects on business morale
- is one of the reasons for accelerating inflation.

Another factor which adversely affects the performance (especially the investment activity) of the Hungarian economy is that of increasing inflation on the year-to-year basis. The CPI was 117.0 per cent in 1989, 128.9 per cent in 1990 and about 135–136 per cent in 1991 (previous

*Table 3.2*   Indicators of involuntary credits

| | Insolvent firms blacklisted[a] by the Hungarian National Bank (HNB) | | Involuntary credits generated[b] by firms not on the HNB blacklist |
|---|---|---|---|
| | Number of firms | Volume of involuntary credit generated[b] (billion HFt) | (billion HFt) |
| | | 1990 | |
| Jan | 176 | 81 | 81 |
| June | 240 | – | 75 |
| Sept | 259 | – | 82 |
| Dec | 282 | 90 | 91 |
| | | 1991 | |
| Jan | 366 | 116 | – |
| March | 413 | 119 | 119 |
| Jun | 481 | 138 | 131 |
| Sept | 620 | 140 | 139 |
| Oct | | | 149 |
| Nov | | | 160 |

*Notes:* [a]i.e. barred from getting credit at commercial banks
[b]i.e. unpaid invoices

year=100 per cent). The picture becomes richer and much more complicated if we use a month-to-month basis. Then, we can see an acceleration of inflation in the second half of 1990, as well. Inflation peaked in January 1991. Since then both the consumer (CPI) and industrial price index (quasi-WPI) have been slowly going down (see table 3.3).

We have to separate the accidental reasons for this slowdown from the impact of business cycle. Among the accidental elements there are the lower than expected oil prices on the world markets, the smaller than expected heating costs borne by households (because of the mild winter), and the unusually low fruit prices (because of the bounteous harvest). It would be misleading to underestimate the impact of these factors, but after 6–7 months of consumer and industrial price indices growing at a slower pace we have to focus on the decelerating impacts of the economic depression as well.

*Table 3.3*    Prices indices (previous month = 100)

| 1991 | CPI | Quasi WPI |
|---|---|---|
| January | 107.5 | 108.1 |
| February | 104.4 | 103.6 |
| March | 103.5 | 101.7 |
| April | 102.4 | 100.6 |
| May | 102.2 | 100.6 |
| June | 102.1 | 100.5 |
| July | 100.9 | 100.9 |
| August | 100.2 | 101.1 |
| September | 101.5 | 100.0 |
| October | 101.3 | 99.9 |
| November | 101.4 | 100.6 |
| December | 101.6 | |
| Jan–Oct | | 133.6 |
| Jan–Nov | 132.2 | |

## RECESSION AND STRUCTURAL CHANGE

Shrinking demand, a growing amount of involuntary credit, and increasing inflation are causes (and at the same time, due to the feedback, the consequences) of the most severe recession in the Hungarian economy since 1956. The GDP, which stagnated in the 1988–89 period, fell by 4.3 per cent in 1990. This tendency has not changed: the expected fall of the GDP in 1991 is 7 per cent. Some Hungarian experts are of the opinion that because of methodological inadequacies the fall may be smaller than that shown by the official statistics. They emphasized that unregistered economic activities were not included in the GDP, therefore the performance of the Hungarian economy was not as bad as the GDP and other official indicators showed. We can not settle this dispute here; instead, let us mention that a number of indicators expressed in physical (non-monetary) units point to the fact that recession has been very deep indeed.

In industry the recession started earlier: industrial production was 99.0 per cent of that in the previous year in 1989, and 90.8 per cent in 1990. In 1991 the recession in that sector even deepened: industrial production in the January–October period was only 79.2 per cent as compared to the same period of 1990. The most serious slump has been registered in such ex-COMECON oriented branches as metallurgy, engineering (especially transport and precision engineering), and textiles. A substantial drop occurred in production of fertilizers and pesticides (58.8 per cent in the period of January–November 1991, compared to the same period of 1990) which also points to serious problems faced by agricultural enterprises.

Agricultural production also declined in the 1989–90 period (97.7 per cent and 89.3 per cent of the production of the preceding year). Despite this decrease, there are product groups where overproduction has been registered (meat, milk, cereals, wine).

Recession seriously affected the construction industry, as well. Its output fell by 15.3 per cent in 1990 and the expected fall for 1991 is in the range of 5–7 per cent. A crisis in the construction industry can also be attributed to the decreased investment activity, as mentioned earlier.

The recession measured in terms of the value of sales is deeper than measured in terms of output produced. In several branches (mostly in agriculture) a huge amount of unsaleable products has accumulated. While the GDP diminished, stocks grew up rapidly (see table 3.4).

*Table 3.4*    Stocks of finished goods in Hungary (previous year = 100 per cent)

| | |
|---|---|
| 1989 | 96.6 |
| 1990 | 119.0 |
| 1991[a] | 150–160 |

*Note:* [a]estimated

Growing unemployment is one of the consequences of the recession (see table 3.5). The number of registered unemployed – which was only 12,064 in 1989 and 89,277 in 1990 – increased rapidly in 1991. There were 406,000 registered unemployed in December 1991. The number of persons receiving unemployment benefits was 130,750 in March and 313,207 in December 1991. The rate of unemployment was 2.5 per cent in December 1990, and a year later, in December 1991, it was already more than 9 per cent.

One has to be cautious with these figures, since there are thousands of people working without being properly registered and accounted for (several thousand foreigners among them) and a lot of registered unemployed are in industry branches, regions, and age groups where the rate of unemployment is much higher than the average. In northeastern Hungary the rate of unemployment is 12–15 per cent or more. The rate of unemployment is also higher than the average among the young and among construction workers.

*Table 3.5*   Level of employment in 1991

|  | first quarter | third quarter |
|---|---|---|
|  | (the same quarter of 1990=100) | |
| Industry | 89.0 | 87.7 |
| Construction | 80.2 | 79.0 |
| Agriculture | 77.8 | 76.4 |
| Transport and communication | 91.7 | |
| Trade | 87.6 | 85.5 |
| Total of the above | 86.1 | 84.6 |

Another consequence of the recession is the decrease in real wage of the majority of the employed (see table 3.6) and a drop in the income of households. Inflation was faster than growth of nominal wages; therefore, in the last four years the real income and/or real wages have been continuously falling.

*Table 3.6*   Real wages in 1986–90 (previous year = 100)

|  | Industry | Agriculture |
|---|---|---|
| 1986 | 101.9 | 102.5 |
| 1987 | 99.6 | 98.2 |
| 1988 | 95.1 | 97.6 |
| 1989 | 100.4 | 96.8 |
| 1990 | 94.9 | 90.1 |

In 1991 the decrease of real wages continued. For example, the growth rate of nominal wages in the industry was 4.5 per cent lower than that of the consumer price index in the January–November period.

There are other signals of growing serious social problems and tensions caused by the long term stagnation and recession. In 1990 the nominal value of the pensions increased by 25.6 per cent. This rate of growth is lower than the CPI growth. People who are not competitive on the changing labour market fear the rapidly growing unemployment. There are signs that the Hungarian middle class is breaking down into two parts, with its majority joining the poor. (This is due to the falling real salaries in health, education, and public administration.) The number of unemployed among the professions grew at a lower rate than the average, but their share among the unemployed reached 16.5 per cent in October 1991. It also means that a growing part of the middle class is not insulated from the unfavourable effects of the transition.

Not unexpectedly, the state enterprises suffered considerably from the impact of deepening recession. As we can see from table 3.7, accumulated losses increased much faster than profits, and, therefore, the financial position of Hungarian state firms (except banks and other financial institutions) worsened considerably.

*Table 3.7*  Net financial position of state enterprises (billion HFt)

| | *Aggregate financial result of firms registering* | | | | *Profits* | | *Change* |
|---|---|---|---|---|---|---|---|
| | *Profits* | | *Losses* | | *(Net)* | | *(Net)* |
| | *1989* | *1990* | *1989* | *1990* | *1989* | *1990* | |
| Firms | 248 | 270 | 26 | 76 | 222 | 194 | -28 |
| Banks and other financial institutions | 84 | 85 | | | 64 | 85 | +21 |
| Together | 312 | 355 | 26 | 76 | 286 | 279 | −7 |

There are signs that the financial position of state owned firms worsened in 1991 as well. As we saw earlier, stocks were growing rapidly in 1991. The main causes of this stockpiling were to be found in the fact that several firms produced without orders from buyers. The production of unsold output was financed mainly by short term loans. Therefore, the stock of those loans grew by 31.5 per cent in the period of January–October 1991. By contrast, the stock of long term credits grew in the same period by only 0.7 per cent. In other words: firms were forced to finance increasing stocks, instead of investment or other profitable ventures.

Another indicator of the worsening financial position of firms is the growing number of liquidation proceedings. As we can see from table 3.8, the number of firms filing for liquidation increased rapidly in 1990 and in the first half of 1991 (see also table 3.9).

Multiple pressures arising out of recession forced some constructive structural changes as well. One of the most important positive effects is that a substantial number of firms made serious and successful efforts to increase their exports to the West. This has been most strongly visible in 1991 when the share of westbound exports (which was 71.8 per cent in 1990) increased to 80.6 per cent in the January–November 1991 period. These structural changes cannot be overlooked, but we

*Table 3.8*   Liquidation proceedings at the Court of Budapest[a]

|  | Number of applications for liquidation | of which, due to insolvency |
|---|---|---|
| 1986 | 5 | |
| 1987 | 71 | 10 |
| 1988 | 144 | 9 |
| 1989 | 384 | 40 |
| 1990 | 630 | 62 |
| 1991 1st half of the year | 528 | 78 |

*Note:* [a]competent to try these cases

*Table 3.9*   Changes in the number of firms on quarterly basis

| | | Total No. of firms | New registrations | Newly established firms | Liquidations |
|---|---|---|---|---|---|
| 1989 | I | 10811 | 828 | 815 | 98 |
| | II | 11551 | 1385 | 1371 | 53 |
| | III | 12863 | 1598 | 1564 | 54 |
| | IV | 14427 | 828 | 828 | 40 |
| 1990 | I | 15235 | 1950 | 1750 | 99 |
| | II | 17086 | 6340 | 5690 | 170 |
| | III | 23256 | 3631 | 3356 | 187 |
| | IV | 26700 | 2946 | 2694 | 176 |
| 1991 | I | 29470 | 9226 | 7895 | 574 |
| | II | 38122 | 4625 | 4149 | 346 |
| | III | 42401 | 2878 | 2425 | 233 |
| | IV | 47923 | (2984)[a] | (2815)[a] | (107)[a] |

*Note:* [a]October–November 1991 only

have to mention that the volume of total export in constant prices declined by 5–7 per cent in 1991. Another unfavourable phenomenon is that in the second part of the year trade – positive in 1989 and 1990 – turned negative in 1991.

The structure of export is practically unchanged. Export-oriented branches – agriculture, engineering, metallurgy – maintained their respective shares. (The only remarkable change is a growing share of the food industry.) We may interpret the geographical shift in sales without changes in the structure of exports as a forced adjustment of state-owned firms and co-operatives to negative effects of falling demand from ex-COMECON countries, as well as to the fall in domestic demand. In the majority of cases these are the same firms, using the same assets, which are selling the same goods elsewhere.

Another positive aspect of the transition is the behaviour of other economic agents: of those in the Hungarian society who have some entrepreneurial skills. A look at table 3.9 reveals a very high rate of formation of new firms.

*Table 3.10* Westbound trade by groups of countries in current prices (in HFt) (previous year or the same period of the previous year = 100)

|  | | *Exports* | |
| --- | --- | --- | --- |
|  | *Total* | *EEC* | *EFTA* |
| 1989 | 116.1 | 127.0 | 125.0 |
| 1990 | 105.6 | 136.8 | 119.0 |
| 1991 Jan–Nov | 117.8 | 146.5 | 141.8 |
|  | | *Imports* | |
| 1989 | 113.7 | 127.9 | 126.3 |
| 1990 | 104.0 | 111.2 | 115.8 |
| 1991 Jan–Nov | 149.3 | 153.7 | 180.5 |
| | *Trade balance (billion of HFt)* | | |
| 1989 | | | + 47.8 |
| 1990 | | | + 58.7 |
| 1991 Jan–Nov | | | − 105.3 |

There were temporary slowdowns in the process, but generally, in the last two years – and especially since the general elections in April 1990 – the number of firms has increased rapidly. Many new firms were established by artisans. This is privatization *par excellence.*

By contrast, in the case of the newly established joint-stock companies, the main stockholder is very often a state-owned firm, bank or state agency.

By July 1991, there were 52 former state-owned firms where the privatization initiated by the State Property Agency (SPA) was concluded. The SPA remained the dominant owner after the transformation of these firms. The Agency had 64.4 per cent of stock in these firms, while the share of foreign investors was only 19.7 per cent. In the same period there were 40 other unfinished cases, where SPA, as the owner of 45.3 per cent of stock, plays a dominant role. Among other stockholders there are state banks, co-operatives, insurance companies, local governments, and private individuals. This dispersal of shares reflects the fact that transformation of a state-owned firm into several joint-stock companies, where the main stockholder is a former state-owned company or the SPA, is not privatization in the proper sense. It is something between decentralization of state property and privatization. More importantly, however, in all the above cases, new decision-makers, owners and managers, try harder to find ways to reduce unfavourable effects of transition than is the case in traditional state-owned enterprises.

As far as foreign investment is concerned, the number of joint ventures was 5,693 at the end of 1990. The value of their assets was 274 billion forints (the share of the foreign investment in these joint ventures was about 34 per cent). The founding spree continued in 1991: the number of newly established joint ventures was 4,098 in the January – October 1991 period. The value of assets of these new firms was 103 billion forints, of which the share of foreign investment was 37.9 per cent (somewhat higher than in 1990). More importantly, the volume of foreign investment has increased very rapidly in the past three years: from 23 million US $ in 1988 to 215 million in 1989, and 569 million US $ in 1990. The volume of foreign direct investment grew very rapidly also in 1991: it was 904 million of US $ in June and the expected value at the end of the year is 1.5 billion.

The presence of the new private sector share is highly visible on several markets. It also creates a lot of new jobs. Among firms with less than 300 employees, the number of employed increased significantly in the first half of 1991. Larger firms, however, registered net job losses.

Worth noting is the change in savings patterns of the population. To counterbalance the negative impact of growing inflation and the negative rate of interest, many households try to preserve or increase the value of savings through shifts in their portfolios (see table 3.11). Many Hungarian households reduced their forints holdings but increased those in foreign currencies and invested in domestic securities (bonds and stocks).

There are, however, serious limits to the investment activity of households. One of them is the households' saving potential. Total savings of the population (including cash and insurance premiums) grew in the first eight months of 1991 by only 16.2 per cent. This is less than the rate of inflation in the period in question. We have also to signal that in real terms households obtained much less credit than before. Another barrier to households' investment activity is the cautious attitude of a large part of the better-off Hungarian who assume the

*Table 3.11* Structure of households' savings in billion HFt

|  | 1988 | 1989 | 1990 | 1991 Oct 31 |
|---|---|---|---|---|
| Domestic currency savings | 283 | 287 | 262 | 291 |
| Foreign currencies savings | 21 | 32 | 72 | 103 |
| Securities |  |  | 96 | 163 |

classical 'wait and see' attitude. They prefer to save than to invest directly in non-financial assets.

Moreover, setting up new firms or changing the savings portfolio, are activities characteristic mostly of the middle class. The lower strata of Hungarian society respond to the recession in other ways. We have no statistical data about the expansion of the 'second', non-registered, or illegal economy, but many observers noted in the last two years a rapid increase in street peddling and the illegal use of state-owned assets (equipment, parts and components) by employees of state-owned firms.

Positive effects of the 'second' economy are well-known. Second economy often creates competitive markets with lower prices or better services. It may diminish the ill-effects of (official) unemployment and may increase GDP as well. All these effects alleviate to some extent the recent recession. But especially in a period of transition to the market economy we cannot forget about the unfavourable effects of the second economy. Those who work there do not pay taxes and social insurance contributions. They use state-owned assets free of charge. This be-haviour violates the rules of fair competition and thus hinders the development of the market economy.

## ECONOMIC POLICY IN ACTION

The new government has never explicitly declared its macroeconomic priorities. On the contrary, all the programmes including the most recent one (the so-called Kupa plan) stressed simultaneous tackling of the major problems without specifying the inevitable trade-offs. There are various reasons for this pragmatic–eclectic economic philosophy of the present Hungarian government. We have to distinguish here between the conditions prevailing in 1990 and in 1991.

In 1990, important steps which had been taken by the former

communist regime limited the room for manoeuvring of the new government. The state budget for 1990 was already passed by the former parliament and the agreement with the IMF and the bilateral agreement with the Soviet Union were signed by the former government.

Another important factor which shaped the economic policy of the government in 1990 was that there was no homogenous team of experts led by a strong personality in the government (unlike in Poland and Czecho-Slovakia). Ministers and advisers responsible for economic affairs belonged to different economic schools and displayed different policy preferences. Some of them argued in favour of a supply side economic policy with a strong state participation. Another group believed in monetary restriction combined with a kind of 'shock therapy'.

After months of hidden and open debates within the government, in December 1990 the Prime Minister invited an expert (at that time not politically affiliated), Mihaly Kupa, to become the new minister of finance. Kupa presented his economic programme only in March 1991. It was a programme that concentrated on macroeconomic stabilization. Since then, the government has prepared only a preliminary version of its policy with respect to structural change.

Kupa's philosophy is an eclectic combination of ideas declared by his debating predecessors. He and his team rejected the shock therapy and supply side economics, but accepted the monetary restriction with a moderately strong state participation in important economic affairs.

Continuing debates of 1991 showed that Kupa and his team were only one of several powerful groups existing within the government and/or coalition parties. For example, Dr Béla Kàdàr, the Minister of International Relations, also promoted economic concepts. They were based on strong state intervention in structural policy and on export promotion. Powerful MPs belonging to the Democratic Forum founded the so called 'Monopoly Group', which lobbyed for faster privatization and for more radical changes in top management of the state-owned enterprises. In other words, not only in the past, but still today there exist different philosophies shaping the economic policies of the government. Under these circumstances we are unable to compare government's preferences and actual decisions.

There have been, however, strongly accentuated priorities of the Antall government displayed throughout the whole period under consideration. They were:

1  to maintain the creditworthiness of the country
2  to slow down the rate of inflation
3  to reduce the growing deficit of the budget.

In the previous survey we listed another priority of the government: to stop the growing surplus in the trade with the Soviet Union. This problem – very important in 1990 – lost its importance after the shift to convertible currency in Hungarian trade with the USSR. Other problems emerged, however, associated with the collapse of the Soviet Union in 1991. Hungarian–Soviet trade radically declined in 1991. The Hungarian government negotiated with the governments of the successor states the new or renewed bilateral agreements referring to a much smaller scale. It is an open question what will happen to the huge Hungarian surplus. These problems have not been solved but – because of their declining importance – they are not anymore among the top priorities of the government.

## Maintaining the creditworthiness

The three above-mentioned priorities reflect the fact that the government and the leaders of the National Bank realized that insolvency, hyperinflation, and an unbalanced state budget may produce serious social tensions which could threaten not only the functioning of the government, but the existence of the whole new democratic order.

As far as the international creditworthiness is concerned, preserving the image of Hungary as a reliable debtor was one of the important goals of the communist government. The new government followed this principle and declared that Hungary stands ready to continue servicing its debt in the future. In this respect, the Hungarian financial management was largely successful. The convertible currency foreign debt did not grow in 1990. This tendency continued in the first ten months of 1991, as well. As table 3.12 reveals, gross foreign debt diminished somewhat in this period.

The structure of the debt has improved, too (the share of the long term loans grew larger). In 1990 this happened, however, at the price of markedly reduced reserves. The share of the long-term loans increased in 1991, too. But this time the amount of reserves remarkably increased (in the period of January–October 1991).

*Table 3.12*    Foreign debt and reserves 1988–91 (in billion US $)

|  | 1988 | 1989 | 1990 | 1991 Jan–Oct |
|---|---|---|---|---|
| Gross foreign debt | 19602 | 20390 | 21270 | 20902 |
| By maturity: |  |  |  |  |
| Short term | 3363 | 3306 | 2941 | 1819 |
| Long and medium term | 16239 | 17084 | 18329 | 19083 |
| International reserves |  |  |  |  |
| Convertible currencies | 1976 | 1725 | 1166 | 3215 |
| of which, in: |  |  |  |  |
| Gold | 510 | 479 | 97 | 79 |
| Foreign exchange | 1467 | 1246 | 1069 | 3136 |
| Other foreign assets in conv. currencies | 4162 | 4434 | 4757 | 4179 |

The reason for this increase may be identified as:

- the fast growth of foreign direct investment
- the unexpectedly high inflow of unilateral transfers
- and (partly in connection with the above developments) the positive balance of payments in convertible currencies (see table 3.13).

*Table 3.13*    Balance of payments in convertible currencies (millions of US $)

|  | 1988 | 1989 | 1990 | 1991 Jan–Oct |
|---|---|---|---|---|
| Current account balance | -807 | -1437 | 127 | 370 |
| Overall balance | 36 | -70 | -562 | 2190 |

## Anti-inflationary measures

The government has declared the level of 38 per cent as the upper acceptable limit of inflation in 1991. The result is better: as we have noted earlier, inflation was 35–36 per cent on a year-to-year basis. This success is a consequence of both spontaneous processes and governmental policies.

We stressed earlier that it was not so much the policy measures taken but mainly the recession itself that slowed down the pace of inflation. We have to add, that the more than satisfactory export performance (more exactly, the surplus on the balance of payments) increased the room for manoeuvre for government's and National Bank's anti-inflationary policy. In other words, the monetary authorities were not forced to devalue the Hungarian forint immediately. On the contrary: the forint was allowed to appreciate in 1991 (there was a devaluation at the end of the year but it only diminished rather than fully offset the effects of the spontaneous appreciation). This postponement of devaluation reduced the rate of inflation.

To counterbalance the foregoing inflationary effects, the National Bank tried to reduce the money stock. The tight money policy was successful: the rate of growth of the money supply was 10 per cent slower than the rate of inflation. Another measure restraining the Hungarian economy was the increase of the required reserve ratio of the banks.

*Table 3.14* Budget balance: planned and actual (in billion of forints)

| Year | | Surplus (+) or Deficit (−) |
|------|------------|------------|
| 1988 | (actual) | − 19.7 |
| 1989 | (planned) | − 21.1 |
| | (actual) | − 54.0 |
| 1990 | (planned) | − 10.0 |
| | (actual) | − 1.4 |
| 1991 | (planned) | − 78.8 |
| | (actual) | − 114.6 |

## Balancing the state budget

The budget balance was very unfavourable in June–July of 1990 (i.e. at the time when the government was formed). The expected year-end deficit was 30–60 billion forints – clearly beyond the limits established by the agreement with the IMF. But deficit of the budget was skilfully reduced by a package of government-introduced measures (reduction of subsidies, increase in consumer taxes).

The successful balancing of the budget in 1990 had, however, some inflationary side effects. This was because firms raised their prices in response to reductions in subsidies and to tax increases. The demand constraint on enterprises was not, in fact, very strong in this period. This was one of the reasons for the increase of the rate of inflation in the second part of 1990.

In 1991, we could observe opposite tendencies. The National Bank's anti-inflationary policy continued. Not only the money supply, but also the amount of loans aimed to finance the budgetary deficit grew relatively slowly (see table 3.15).

*Table 3.15*   Monetary developments 1990–1 (billion HFt)

| | Money supply (M2) | Budget deficit financed by the Central Bank | Deposits of banks | firms |
|---|---|---|---|---|
| 1990 Jan 31 | 699.9 | 420.9 | 77.2 | 171.1 |
| 1990 Jun 30 | 740.5 | 417.9 | 222.2 | 193.0 |
| 1990 Oct 31 | 817.9 | 470.4 | 244.6 | 253.0 |
| 1991 Jan 1 | 912.5 | 468.9 | 293.8 | 285.5 |
| 1991 Jan 31 | 892.0 | 508.9 | 335.0 | 271.5 |
| 1991 Feb 28 | 905.4 | 508.9 | 342.1 | 279.0 |
| 1991 Oct 31 | 1024.9 | 542.6 | 465.8 | 304.4 |
| 1991 Oct 31 (1990 Oct 31 =100) | 125.3 | 115.3 | 190.4 | 120.3 |

Under the pressure of this growing monetary squeeze (and of the shrinking demand), the increase of prices was in 1991 lower than many firms had expected. As we saw earlier, a consequence of this was the worsening liquidity position of many firms. Of course, enterprises tried to offset the negative effects of their worsening financial position. They made redundant a part of the working population – the negative side-effect of this is the growing unemployment. Another method of avoiding the liquidity crisis was tax evasion. The effect is clear: the revenue of the state budget was much less than planned. Thus, it was a lower revenue rather than excessive spending that produced the huge deficit of the 1991 budget.

The performance of the Hungarian economic leadership, as measured by the fulfilment of their own priorities, was not bad in 1990–1. A stabilized foreign debt, no hyperinflation, and a balanced budget (in 1990 but not in 1991) should be considered as a real success. However, if we use other success indicators, like the change in GDP, unemployment, or the level of real wages, the performance is not so impressive.

Moreover, in 1991 the macroeconomic indicators have been deteriorating with time. There is growing unemployment and a deepening recession in industry and agriculture.

And here lies the dilemma for the Hungarian economic leadership. If they wanted to decrease unemployment, stimulate growth, and increase the revenue of the budget and of the households, they would have to revitalize the whole economy. But how can they revitalize it without letting inflation increase and how can they avoid deterioration of the balance of payments at the same time?

## TRANSITION

The performance of the Hungarian economy or the quality of economic policy-making are measured not only by macroeconomic and microeconomic indicators. The general public's attention both in and outside East Central Europe focuses on the systemic changes. The real success would be a relatively smooth and quick transition from the reformed Soviet-type economy to a market economy – combined with the shift from a totalitarian regime to a Western-type political democracy.

We shall focus here only on two aspects of the transition: on institutional changes in the narrower sense of the word and on changes in property rights (privatization).

### Institutional changes

An important change in the institutional framework of the Hungarian economy is the new and growing role of the parliament in the regulation and control of the macroeconomic sphere. The rubber-stamp quasi-parliament of the communist past is over. There are powerful parliamentary committees, such as the budgetary or the economic one which are deeply involved not only in the preparation of new laws, but in controlling economic processes as well. Of course, conflicts often arise between parliamentary committees and the government officials. They arise mostly because of the lack of information, but this is more of a norm when economic policy-making takes place in a decentralized setting.

The role of the parliament as a whole has increased. There are meaningful debates on economic issues. Also the parliamentary hearings are an effective form of control and critique of the governmental activity.

The government structure has changed. The former branch ministries and the powerful Central Planning Office are gone, and new ministries have been created. The Ministry of International Economic Relations has been formed. Another new one is the Ministry of Industry and Trade. Subordinated to the latter is the new Small Business Office. A new governmental agency is the Office of Competition responsible for the anti-trust regulation of the Hungarian economy. The former State Committee of Labour and Wages became the Ministry of Labour.

The State Property Agency is responsible for privatization of the state sector. Another new institution is emerging: the State Property Holding that will supervise the enterprises remaining in state hands. There are new ministers without portfolio who are responsible for economic affairs. One is supervising all the banks, another is responsible for privatization, and still another is dealing with the land reform. Unfortunately, the expected and promised reduction of the state administration did not come about. On the contrary: the number of those employed by the central state administration grew in 1990–1.

Not only the management of the state but the institutions of the civil society have changed. There are several new organizations of ethnic minorities, environmentalists, pensioners, etc. As far as the economy is concerned, there are several newly established or formed employers' and employees' organizations. With respect to the former, a network of old and new organizations tries to articulate and defend interests of entrepreneurs and managers. But in spite of their loud and sometimes aggressive lobbying, the majority of the self-employed did not join these organizations.

The situation is a bit different on the side of the employed. There are new independent trade unions and workers' councils but these organizations represent only a minority of the employed. On the other hand, there exist associations of the old 'reformed' (originally established under the communist regime) trade unions. There are about 1.5 million registered members of these unions. They control all the assets of the former trade union 'movement' and this is one of the reasons why they survived the collapse of the communist regime: the benefits offered to members by the old trade unions are usually better than those offered by the new ones. Another possible reason for their continued viability may be that elections in these unions have been postponed so far.

Because of the aggressive competition among unions and among entrepreneurial organizations, and because of the huge number of people which are not under the umbrella of any of those organizations, the system of intermediation between various interest groups is very weak in Hungary. The mediating body established for this purpose and subordinated to the government does not have enough power. Therefore, in a spontaneous revolt such as the nationwide blockade of roads by taxi drivers and other extremist groups in October 1990, it is very difficult to establish credible *ad hoc* machinery of negotiation.

## Privatization

We have already noted how fast was the increase of the number of (mainly) private firms in Hungary. In this respect the privatization 'from below' goes fast. But what about privatization 'from above', i.e. transforming the state sector into a privately-owned one? All main political parties and organizations agree on the need of privatization of the huge state sector. In spite of their consensus more than 90 per cent of the assets are still in the hands of the state or of the big co-operatives.

No doubt, there are serious technical, financial, and even ideological barriers to the privatization. Moreover, the lack of required knowledge and the resistance of some social groups hinder the process as well. A public opinion poll has showed that 27 per cent of the population was against the privatization of state-owned firms in January 1991. Five months later, the share of opponents increased to 34 per cent. The share of opponents is higher in the case of privatization of the firm they are working in (55–60 per cent). There are very strong sentiments against the foreign investors and more than 70 per cent of people asked opposed the restoration of large estates to the former owners. The main reason for this negative attitude is that a lot of people are afraid of unemployment.

Another group of opponents is involved in various illegal, 'second' economy activities. Many of them prefer to remain in the illegal business since it seems to them less risky than to establish a new (legal) private firm. On the one hand, they do not pay taxes, social security contributions, etc. On the other hand, those who use state-owned assets (machinery, materials, parts, components, etc.) in their illegal activities know perfectly well that this type of parasitism, tolerated in state-owned firms, will be quickly terminated in firms with 'real' owners. Therefore, they prefer the status quo.

The foregoing largely explains why privatization is progressing at a slow speed. But on top of all the problems referred to above, some government policy failures add to the complexity and slowness of the process in question. There were two centrally managed privatization programmes of the government.

The first privatization programme included twenty big and medium-size state-owned firms with assets evaluated at 33 billion forints. It started in September 1990. Half a year later, consulting firms were selected but there was no agreement between the advisory firms, privatized firms, and the State Property Agency that finalizes the privatization procedure.

As we mentioned earlier, the number of big and medium-size firms' whose privatization by the SPA was completed by June 1990, was only 52. There were another 96 firms in which the process of privatization has started. We have to add that there are about 2,200 state-owned firms in Hungary. The book value of these 52 privatized firms was 45.3 billion forints. It is about 2–3 per cent of the book value of all state-owned firms.

Another centrally managed privatization programme is that in which about 10,000 stores and restaurants were offered for sale or lease. Half a year later the minister responsible for this action could inform the parliament about the successful privatization of only 200 stores and restaurants. In the second half of 1991 realization of this programme speeded up, and at the end of the year some 2,100 stores and restaurants were sold or leased.

A part of retail trade and catering-trade companies involved tried to avoid privatization. Also, the delay in forming a special fund for financing small scale privatization hindered the governmental actions. But the main reason is the over-centralization of privatization itself.

The establishment of the State Property Agency was a response of the government to the so-called spontaneous privatization, which was heavily criticized by the whole opposition to the communist regime. Moreover, it was the rejection of a concept of the liberals whose slogan: 'privatization of the privatization', was unacceptable to the voters of the conservative–nationalist coalition.

But the Agency, employing about 200 persons, is technically unable to deal with hundreds of cases. The Agency has conflicting success indicators: it is impossible to maximize the revenue from privatization and to maximize the price of every transaction at the same time.

The new minister of finance has realized these weaknesses of the governmental privatization and – in tacit agreement with the liberal opposition – proposed the introduction of methods based on active participation of managers of firms interested in privatization. There are, however, political obstacles to privatization caused by conflicting aims of the coalition partners. The two small parties of the coalition are not privatization- but restitution-oriented. The programme of the Smallholders Party is very simple: to give back the property (in particular the land) to the original owners. The main political target of the Christian Democratic Party is to restore church property confiscated by communists. Both aims carry high economic risk. The restitution is very time-consuming and may have a substantial inflationary impact. Experts of the Democratic Forum recognized these dangers, and the one-year history of the coalition was the story of compromises between political targets and economic rationality. In May and June of 1991 political aims prevailed: the parliament passed both laws of restitution. In the second half of 1991 privatization became faster: the privatization revenue received by the budget was 600 million forints in 1990 and 31 billion forints in 1991.

*Table 3.16* Annual data on Hungarian economy (previous year =, or the same period of the previous year = 100 per cent)

|  | 1988 | 1989 | 1990 | 1991 |
|---|---|---|---|---|
| GDP | 99.9 | 100.2 | 95.7 | 93* |
| Industrial production | 100.0 | 96.6 | 95.0 | 87* |
| Construction | 96.8 | 100.8 | 84.1 | 95* |
| Agriculture | 104.3 | 97.7 | 89.3 | |
| Consumption private** | 96.0 | 101.9 | 95.5 | 94* |
| public | | 94.2 | 99.4 | |
| Investment (unchanged prices) | 89.9 | 97.3 | 91.3 | 90* |
| Investment fixed capital (buildings/machines) total (current prices) | | 116.0 | 97.2 | |
| Investment total capital industrial | 92.9 | 99.0 | 100.0 | |
| Inventories, total | | 74.5 | 85.7 | |
| Employment (prod.) | 96.9 | 95.5 | 90.2 | 86.1 (J-M) |
| industry | 97.4 | 96 | 90.9 | 84.1 (J-O) |
| agriculture | 93.7 | 93.1 | 88.2 | |
| Unemployment (no. of persons) | | 12064 | 89284 | 406000 |
| Rate of unemployment | | | 2.5 | 9.1 |
| Number of firms | 9597 | 10811 | 15235 | 47923 |
| from this new ones | 1377 | 4578 | 13491 | 2878 (Oct) |
| Wages and salaries (income in real terms) | 98.7 | 102.5 | 98.4 | |
| industry (wages in nominal terms) | 108.6 | 111.0 | | 132.2 (Oct) |
| Consumer prices | 115.5 | 117.0 | 128.9 | 135.2 (Dec) |
| Households' income | | 116.9 | 129.9 | 123.0 |
| Households' savings rate | | 104.6 | 119.1 | |

| Retail trade sales | 94.7 | 99.8 | | 75.4 (Sept) |
|---|---|---|---|---|
| **Monetary and fiscal data** | | | | |
| Money supply on M2 basis | | | | 125.3 |
| Interest rate charged by commercial | 19.1– | 19.8– | | |
| banks | 23.0 | 26.6 | | |
| Credit expansion firms and co-operatives | | 450.8 | 539.9 | |
| population (billions of HUF) | | | | |
| Credits for private non-agricultural sector | | 18.5 | 42.7 | |
| **International economic relations** | | | | |
| Convertible | | | | |
| export | 5505 | 6444 | 6346 | 4320 (J–Jun) |
| import | 5016 | 5910 | 5998 | 4494 (J–Jun) |
| balance of foreign trade (million US$) | 489 | 537 | 348 | −144 (J–Jun) |
| Non convertible | | | | |
| export | 4484 | 4047 | 2719 | 418 (J–Jun) |
| import | 4390 | 3540 | 2529 | 188 (J–Jun) |
| balance of foreign trade (million US$) | 94 | 507 | 190 | 230 (J–Jun) |
| Imports of capital goods | | | | |
| Balance of payments | | | | |
| convertible (million US$) | −807 | −1437 | 127 | −112 (J–Jun) |
| non convertible | 233 | 866 | 250 | 216 (J–Jun) |
| Brutto foreign debt (million US$) | | | | |
| convertible | 19625 | 20605 | 21270 | 19727 (J-Jun) |
| non convertible | 583 | 361 | 235 | 186 (J-Jun) |
| Exchange rates to | | | | |
| US $ (Ft/100 US $) | 5042 | 5909 | 6319 | 7710 |
| DMark (Ft/ 100 DM) | 2873 | 3146 | 3914 | 4555 |

*Notes:* * 1991 estimated
       ** consumption of the population

# 4 Polish survey

*Michal Zielinski*

## MAIN INDICATORS DESCRIBING THE MACROECONOMIC SITUATION IN POLAND IN 1991

The picture of the Polish economy in 1991, as given by main economic indicators, is a disastrous one (see table 4.1). GDP went down by 7 per cent, investment fell by about 10 per cent (in the previous year it decreased by 10 per cent, too), and consumption was stagnant (in 1990 it dropped by 15 per cent). Unemployment nearly doubled during 1991 and the unemployment rate increased rapidly from 6 per cent of the labour force at the beginning of the year to over 10 per cent at the end

*Table 4.1* Main economic indicators in 1991 rate of change in real terms (1990 = 100)

| | |
|---|---|
| GDP | 93 |
| Industrial output | 85 |
| Investment | 90 |
| Consumption | 97 |
| Average wage[a] | 104 |
| Unemployment[b] | 191 |
| Export | 94 |
| Import | 134 |
| Money supply (in nominal terms)[b,c] | 158 |
| CPI | 170 |
| Budget balance[d] | − 0.14 |

*Notes:* [a]in six sectors of economy (industry, construction, transport, communication and community services)
[b]end of 1991/end of 1990 ratio
[c]M-2
[d]balance/expenditure ratio
*Source:* Central Statistical Office (GUS)

of 1991. The only good economic news were the balanced foreign trade and a decrease in the inflation rate.

However, even these relatively optimistic results cannot be treated as an unqualified success. A moderate increase in exports coexisted with a rapid growth in imports. Inflation, as measured by CPI on a year-by-year basis, fell from almost 700 per cent in 1990 to 70 per cent in 1991 but it still remained high. To make matters worse, the budget deficit was on the increase and threatened the reacceleration of inflation.

But this is a picture of an economy that is only skin deep. At a closer look, a different picture could be seen. Atypically for an economy in crisis, the average wage in real terms was about 4 per cent higher than a year before. The number of registered private cars (a rather typical measure of welfare) increased by 700,000, i.e. by 15 per cent. The number of TV sets, videos and PCs increased rapidly as well.

Although the fact of recession is not questioned in this survey, a fair assessment of the complex phenomenon of the economy in transition is in order. The above-mentioned data deal only with a part of the economy. Central Statistical Office is monitoring and publishing current data with respect only to larger – both state-owned and private – enterprises.[1] The registered small businesses are outside regular data collection.[2] Needless to say, the same applies to the whole 'informal' sector. Therefore, the statistics underestimate the size of the output and of many other economic indicators. An unwelcome consequence is that all analyses should contain a disclaimer 'errors and omissions included'. An efficient system of collecting data and (what is worse) taxes has not been created during the first two years of reforms.

The non-agricultural aggregate output recorded by GUS (see note 1) fell in 1991 by about 14 per cent. While output stagnated in the construction sector, the overall fall was mainly due to output decreases in transportation (by 25 per cent) and in industry (by 14 per cent). The recession affected all the sectors of industry (see table 4.2).

The sharp fall in output was accompanied by an even sharper decrease in profitability. Gross financial result (gross profit) in enterprises decreased in 1991 in nominal terms by more than 50 per cent and was lower than the nominal value of taxes which enterprises paid a year before. As a result, enterprises did not fully pay their taxes (at the end of the 1991 year the arrears were over 25 trillion zl.), which contributed to the rising budget deficit. Arrears apart, taxes effectively paid by enterprises absorbed all their profits, and the sphere of production as a whole ended last year with a negative net profit rate.

*Table 4.2*   Output in 1991: real rate of change[a]

|                       | 1990=100 | 1989=100 |
|-----------------------|----------|----------|
| Output total          | 86.0     | 71.8     |
| Industry total        | 85.8     | 65.1     |
| Food                  | 99.5     | 75.9     |
| Mineral               | 92.0     | 72.2     |
| Fuel and power        | 91.6     | 71.3     |
| Chemical              | 85.4     | 64.4     |
| Metallurgical         | 80.3     | 62.3     |
| Electro-engineering   | 73.9     | 57.6     |
| Light                 | 81.4     | 53.9     |
| Construction sector   | 99.0     | 85.0     |
| Transportation sector | 75.0     | 64.5     |

*Note:* [a]deflated by price index of industrial production
*Source:* see Table 4.1

In 1991 the fiscal drain hit the relatively better enterprises. On the other hand, the share of loss-making enterprises in the total increased to 39 per cent (21 per cent in 1990). These SOEs continued to exist due to state banks' new and consolidated credits and delayed payments for deliveries to other SOEs and private firms (probably delayed *ad calendas Graecas*). This created a chain of involuntary credits and was responsible for the fictitiousness of profitability data of Polish large state-owned commercial banks, as many of those SOEs also owed money to these banks. A sizeable share of the latter will most probably never be repaid.

## MONETARY POLICY AND ITS IMPACT ON AGGREGATE DEMAND

What were the reasons for output fall and the financial collapse of enterprises? The simplest and the most common theory is that the restrictive monetary policy throttled internal demand.[3] This way of thinking might be summarized as follows. The insufficient money supply resulted in the demand fall for consumer goods and for capital goods (both directly and indirectly through increase in the interest rate). This caused the decrease in output and the increase in average costs with negative consequences for gross profits and budgetary revenue. The rise in tax rate necessary to restore budgetary balance reduced net profits and had a negative influence on the output. The positive conclusion drawn from such a chain of reasoning is to create additional money injections which would revitalize domestic demand and put the economy onto the growth path.

A simple test fails to confirm this reasoning. Money supply (M2) increased in 1991 by 58.3 per cent, total output by 26.6 per cent, output in industry by 26.2 per cent (all data in nominal terms) and industrial prices by 47.2 per cent. Moreover, it might be shown, by including the time factor, that output was perversely correlated with money supply. The last quarter of 1991 was the only one in which there was a rise in nominal total output (to 256 trillion zl.). During four previous quarters, output was by and large stable and amounted to 235 trillion zl.). However, this quarter was the only one in which there was a sharp reduction in rate of change in money supply (M2 increased by 4.5 per cent while in four previous quarters this rate amounted to 15 per cent).

Three objections could be raised to the above analysis. First, the analysis is based on nominal data, it deals with rather long periods of time (quarters) and treats output as a function of only one variable (money). Therefore, in table 4.3, I present the rates of change in real supply of money and corrected real output in industry in 1991 on a month-to-month basis.

*Table 4.3*   Rates of change in money supply (M2) and industrial output in 1991 (on monthly basis)

|  | Money supply | | Industrial output | |
|  | *Nominal* | *Real[a]* | *Real[a]* | *Corrected[b]* |
|---|---|---|---|---|
| | | *Rate of change* | | |
| January | +9,8 | −7,0 | −17,6 | −7,6 |
| February | +7,5 | +2,0 | +0,8 | −2,7 |
| March | +7,5 | +6,0 | +0,1 | −3,4 |
| April | +7,4 | +6,3 | −8,3 | −4,2 |
| May | +3,3 | +1,6 | −1,3 | −2,0 |
| June | +3,3 | +0,2 | +2,2 | −2,8 |
| July | +5,4 | +3,2 | −12,1 | +2,8 |
| August | +3,8 | +2,1 | +5,9 | +1,8 |
| September | +3,1 | −1,5 | +3,5 | +2,2 |
| October | +1,8 | −0,5 | +1,3 | +2,8 |
| November | +0,5 | −0,5 | +5,9 | +1,0 |
| December | +1,0 | −0,5 | −4,5 | −7,7 |

*Notes:* [a]deflated by price index of industrial production
[b]effective output in comparable working time corrected by coefficient of seasonal fluctuations in output.
*Source:* see table 4.1. Corrected production data were published by Marek Misiak: 'Smutny bilans' (A Sad Balance), *Życie Gospodarcze*, 26 January 1992

The thesis I would like to present here is not that there was no connection between changes in money supply and output. I argue that there is no evidence that the insufficient money supply was the only (or the main) cause of economic recession. I suppose that important sources of fall in output should be looked for somewhere else. The monetary policy also mattered, but the influence of this factor was far more intricate.

The first interesting fact which can be noted here concerns money stock in possession of economic units. In spite of expanding total money supply, money stock of enterprises declined strongly. At the end of 1989, the share of total money stock in possession of economic units amounted to 33 per cent. At the end of the next year this share dropped to 29 per cent and at the end of 1991 to only 25.6 per cent. Firms' real money stock fell during two years by half. Through the period there has been a redistribution of money stock from enterprises to households (both directly and via the budget and its social security transfers). The main characteristic features of monetary policy in 1991 were an increasing share of the budget demand for money and both absolutely and relatively high interest rates combined with excess demand for credits. The state budget participated there in two ways. First (see table 4.4), by financing its deficit with credit from the National Bank of Poland it increasingly crowded out the enterprises of the credit market. Second, the budget joined the enterprise sector in expanding the chain of involuntary credits by delaying payments, mainly to the public services sector. In this way, the budget also initiated creation of additional informal money supply, as institutions dependent on the budget had to

*Table 4.4* Budget deficit and net credit expansion for enterprise sector (economic units) in 1990–1 (in trillion zl.)

|  | *Budget deficit[a]* | *Net credit expansion* | *Budget deficit/Net credit expansion ratio* |
|---|---|---|---|
| IV Quarter '90 | 6,3 | 23,9 | 0,26 |
| I Quarter '91 | 5,0 | 14,1 | 0,35 |
| II Quarter '91 | 8,2 | 19,7 | 0,42 |
| III Quarter '91 | 9,2 | 22,2 | 0,41 |
| IV Quarter '91 | 10,0 | 20,0 | 0,50 |

*Notes:* [a]official data. Taxes amounting to 2.5 trillion zl, which were actually paid by enterprises in the first quarter of 1991, had been calculated as budgetary revenues in the last quarter of 1990.
*Source: Informacja o sytuacji gospodarczej kraju* (GUS), May 1991. Data for the last quarter of 1991 are provisional

postpone their payments to others in the chain of indebtment.[4]

The Balcerowicz plan's concept of monetary policy was that interest rate should be an equilibrium price of money. A very high initial nominal level of interest rate should eliminate excess demand for credit. As a result of positive selection of borrowers according to the efficient use of money criterion, a higher price of money should not have anti-inflationary consequences. After this first stage, in which the interest rate should clear the money market, it would constantly fall in parallel with the drop in inflation rate.

Contrary to expectations, interest rate did not fulfil this task. It was all the time at a high – even if fluctuating – level and ironically, in spite of being high, it was not the equilibrium price. There was only slight improvement (if any) in the credit structure. As a result, the interest rate fed rather than extinguished inflation.

All quantitative conclusions have to be based on the rediscount rate (it might be assessed that the commercial credit rate was about 10–20 per cent higher). Even this rate exceeded WPI (Index of Industrial Production Prices is taken as the closest substitute – see table 4.5).

*Table 4.5*   The rediscount rate and WPI (index of industrial production prices) in 1990–1 (in per cent - annual rate)

|  | *Rediscount annual rate* | *WPI Annual rate* | *Rediscount rate/WPI ratio* |
|---|---|---|---|
| I half of 1990 | 212.0 | 176.3 | 1.20 |
| II half of 1990 | 40.2 | 42.8 | 0.98 |
| I half of 1991 | 64.8 | 55.6 | 1.06 |
| II half of 1991 | 42.9 | 25.0 | 1.14 |

*Source:* see table 4.1

The data from table 4.5 show that the cost of credit increased in real terms in 1991. The credit risk increased as well. Interest rate was not only high but it also changed very rapidly. It had been falling for the first nine months of 1990 and then jumped in the October–December period from 34 per cent to 55 per cent. In January 1991, rather unexpectedly, it was raised again to 72 per cent. This interest rate seesaw put many investors, who had taken credit some months earlier, in a predicament. Moreover, many potential new investors changed their mind and postponed or even cancelled their plans to expand. Hardly anyone could find projects whose predicted profitability rate would be commensurate with so high an interest rate.

Despite the disincentives to invest, demand for credit exceeded supply. The paradox of excess demand for credit was connected with two factors. First, 1991 was the period of credit crunch. Throughout 1991 new credits (increase in credit liabilities, see table 4.4) were smaller than in the last quarter of 1990. Second, there was no positive selection by the market: an overwhelmingly large part of supply was created by state commercial banks and almost as large a part of demand was created by large SOEs. The interest elasticity of SOEs' demand for credit has been close to zero. These 'mammoths of socialist indus-trialization' are commonly regarded as 'too big to go bankrupt' (the best proof of this thesis is the fact that there have been no bankruptcies in this class of enterprises since the beginning of the reform). Credits that these SOEs took were mainly provided not for reconstruction but for continued existence without any further reaching adjustment.

The third group of economic agents participating in the credit market were housing co-operatives. For many years these institutions, supply-ing the bulk of apartment-house based dwellings, were generously subsidized. A rapid reduction of housing subsidies caused a huge increase in the liabilities of these co-operatives.

It must be stressed at this point, that there was a credit crunch but not a monetary squeeze in 1991. Credit diminished (also in nominal terms) but total money stock increased by and large in parallel with the inflation rate. (As a memorandum item: in 1991, on December-to-December basis, M2 in nominal terms increased by 58.3 per cent, CPI by 60 per cent and quasi-WPI by 36.7 per cent.) As stressed already, there was a redistribution, not reduction, of money stock.

The changes in foreign currency reserves could also affect domestic money supply. Data concerning this point (see table 4.6) should be

*Table 4.6* Foreign currency reserves in 1989–91 (nominal value in zlotys and US $ at the end of year)

|  | Foreign Currency Stock | |
|---|---|---|
|  | *in zlotys* (*trillion*) | *in US $[a]* (*billion*) |
| 1989 | 69.5 | 7.3 |
| 1990 | 59.8 | 6.3 |
| 1991 | 67.0 | 6.1 |

*Note:* [a]calculated at the rate (for one US $): 1989 – 9570 zloty (free market rate); 1990 – 9500 zloty (NBP rate); 1991 - 11,072 zloty (NBP rate)
*Source:* see table 4.1

treated with caution. But even these data confirm an intuitive opinion that Poland has probably been an exporter of capital since the beginning of 1990. Some flows could be estimated. For example, large used car imports by individuals cost about 1 billion dollars in 1991 (430 thousand cars at a price – let us say – of 2,000 US dollars per car).[5]

One can speculate that there were other, more sophisticated financial transactions as well. If deposit rate in Poland amounted to 55 per cent per annum in 1991 (at least 40 percentage points better than in EEC countries) and the devaluation rate of the zloty was about 25 per cent, it was easy to calculate that currency transfer to Poland and repatriation of interest gave a net profit rate on such a transaction equal to 15 per cent. Thus, it is highly probable that such transactions in fact took place.

We arrive at a conclusion that monetary policy was inconsistent. It reduced credit supply quite significantly. It encouraged savings through a very strongly positive interest rate but – for that very reason – it discouraged investment. Moreover, it did little to direct financial resources to the enterprise sector of the economy.

## GROSS PROFITABILITY OF OUTPUT: REASONS FOR DECLINE

The above-mentioned redistribution of the money stock (mainly from enterprises to households) could change the structure of demand (by shifting demand from capital to consumer goods) but should not change its size. If there were enough money to create demand for domestic output, what were the reasons for output decline? The fall in demand for domestic output had, in this writer's opinion, a largely autonomous character. 'The mystery of vanishing output' was described in detail by Winiecki.[6] At this point, I would only like to remark that it is impossible to recreate demand by increasing money supply. The only way in which capital goods may be demanded again is the far reaching restructuring of production structure.

In this context, the second cause of the fall in demand should be pointed at. This is known from the former GDR economy as a 'Trabi versus Opel' problem. For the first time Polish enterprises had to compete with the generally superior foreign products. In this competition, they had to make strenuous efforts both to minimize their costs and to make their products more attractive.

Similar efforts have had to be made to restructure Polish exports. The collapse of the Soviet economy forced many enterprises to look for new markets. This was a large-scale problem because of a high share of exports to the former Soviet Union in total exports, which amounted to 31 per cent in 1989 and dropped to 20 per cent in 1990 (in GDP terms it was 4 per cent and 3.3 per cent respectively). In 1991, there was another drop in these exports which reduced its share in total exports to 11 per cent (i.e. 1.5 per cent GDP). The situation of exports to small ex-COMECON countries was even worse. Exports to Romania fell in 1991 by over 80 per cent, to Bulgaria by 75 per cent, and to Hungary by 20 per cent. The only increase was in exports to Czecho-Slovakia: by over 20 per cent (all the above in nominal terms). Total exports to ex-COMECON (including the former Soviet Union) decreased from 30.8 trillion zl. to 25.8 trillion zl., i.e. by 16 per cent in nominal and by 42 per cent in real terms (their share in total export diminished from 21.7 per cent to 11.7 per cent).

The sharp fall of demand from ex-COMECON countries was a tragedy for some enterprises, for example in the armament or aircraft industry, where for obvious reasons they could not find alternative markets. Nonetheless, economy-wise, pro-export orientation advanced. Exports to EEC countries increased in 1991 from 64.3 to 83.6 per cent trillion zl., that is by 30 per cent in nominal and by 16 per cent in real terms. As a result, there was an aggregate increase in total exports in nominal terms and only a small drop in real terms (by 1.4 per cent).

On the other hand, imports increased at much higher rates, overall by 42.5 per cent in nominal and by 35.6 per cent in real terms, with imports from EEC countries increasing at roughly the same rates. Moreover, there was a rapid increase in imports of consumer goods; in the period January–September 1991 on a yearly basis (by 125 per cent), and only a moderate rise in imports of capital goods (by 40 per cent) and materials (by 19 per cent – all three magnitudes in real terms). The share of consumer goods in the total import value rose from 19.3 per cent to over 30 per cent. The incremental imports of consumer goods in 1991 may be estimated at 20 trillion zl., which was equal to 2 per cent of gross domestic output in 1991.

This is one more sign that – first of all – the structure of incentives encouraged consumption rather than investment and – second – that money stock redistribution through monetary and fiscal policy from the production to consumption sphere created demand for imported rather than domestic goods.

Opel has to win economic competition with Trabi. In this sense, the shift in demand from domestic to foreign products is quite natural.

However, the exchange rate policy should promote export and support Polish enterprises on the internal market or be neutral *vis-à-vis* respective inflation rates.

The exchange rate was fixed for more than sixteen months (1 January 1990 to 17 May 1991). Starting from strong undervaluation of the zloty *vis-à-vis* the real US dollar, the zloty became increasingly overvalued (by about 80 per cent). As a result both Polish exports and competitive position of Polish enterprises on the domestic market suffered. The moderate devaluation of the zloty (by 16.8 per cent), which took place in May 1991 could only change this situation to some extent. The new exchange rate policy (the so-called 'crawling peg') introduced on 27 October 1991, seems to be a better one. However, the accepted rate of devaluation of exchange rate fixed at 10 zloty per one working day (50 zloty weekly, 230 zloty or 2 per cent monthly) was still lower than the inflation rate differential. Especially, if we face the reality that due to the structure of 'currency basket' (US dollar 0.45; DM 0.35; British pound 0.1; Swiss and French francs both 0.05 each), dollar depreciation resulted in actual appreciation of the zloty; from 11.453 (end of July 1991) to 11.072 (end of December 1991) per US dollar. Simultaneously, for the first time since the beginning of the reform there was a visible spread (6 per cent) between market and official exchange rates.

In consequence tariffs became the substitute for more devaluation. An average import tariff which had dropped in the first stage of the reform from 13.3 per cent (in 1989) to 8.0 per cent (in 1990) was raised to 18.1 per cent in August 1991. The analysis of tariff policy by Dziewulski showed that it resulted in an increase of prices rather than of domestic output.[7] It indicated SOEs' inclination to profit from their monopolistic positions.

Let me discuss the enterprise profitability problem in greater detail. In table 4.7 I present the components of gross profit calculation. Between 1990 and 1991 there was a decrease in enterprises' subsidies and a moderate increase in turnover tax. Another interesting feature is the rapid deterioration in the balance of financial operations.

A comment should be made on this point. There is nothing abnormal in either the tendency to reduce subsidies in the market economy or to change the level of tax burden. However, the rapid deterioration of the balance of financial operations certainly needs to be explained. As it has been noted by Winiecki,[8] the reduction of SOEs' reserves of foreign currencies was a source of super profits in 1990. (They sold more than $1.7 billion only in the first half of 1990.) In 1991, this

*Table 4.7* Gross financial results in 1990–1 (nominal value in trillion zlotys)[a]

|  | 1990 | 1991 |
|---|---|---|
| Sales' Receipts | 758.2 | 960.0 |
| less: |  |  |
| Costs | 595.3 | 832.0 |
| Equal | 162.9 | 128.0 |
| less: |  |  |
| Turnover Tax | −47.9 | −55.0 |
| plus: |  |  |
| Subsidies | +37.7 | +28.0 |
| Balance of Financial Operations | +22.4 | −35.0 |
| Gross Profits | +175.1 | +72.0 |

*Note:* [a] Central Statistical Office (GUS)

source of increase in their money stocks vanished.

For analytical purposes, I put the balance equation of gross profit in the following form:

$$GP = RO \times WPI \times (1 - AC + ITR + FOR)$$

where:

RO = Real Output (Real Receipts from Sales)
WPI = Wholesale Price Index (Index of Industrial Production Prices)
AC = Average Cost (average 'cost' of unit of receipts or Cost/Receipts Ratio)
ITR = Indirect Tax Rate (Turnover Tax and Subsidies Balance/Receipts Ratio)
FOR = Finance Operation/Receipts Ratio

The parameters of this equation for the years 1990–1 are presented below:

|  | RO | WPI | AC | ITR | FOR |
|---|---|---|---|---|---|
| 1990 | 100.0 | 100.0 | 0.785 | −0.013 | +0.029 |
| 1991 | 86.0 | 147.2 | 0.867 | −0.028 | −0.036 |

According to the immortal *ceteris paribus* assumption, it may be calculated that:

- price increases raised gross profits by 82.7 trillion zl.
- increase in average costs reduced profits by 62.1 trillion zl.

- deterioration in financial operations' results reduced profit by 49.2 trillion zl.
- contraction of output reduced profits by 24.5 trillion zl.
- increase in turnover tax rate and decrease in subsidies reduced profits by 11.4 trillion zl.

This calculation points to the increase in unit costs as a main source of the profit reduction. Average costs which rose by 9.5 per cent in 1991 (in 1990 by 8.3 per cent) in real terms have increased during the last two years at a rather stable quarterly rate (*c.* 2 per cent). The only exception was the first quarter of 1991, when cost increases accelerated.

A much steeper increase in costs in the first quarter of 1991 can easily be explained. It was caused by a massive rise in the prices of fuel and energy. In January 1991, as compared with December 1990, natural gas became dearer by 60 per cent, coal and coke by 25 per cent, electricity by 15 per cent and fuel oil by 12 per cent.

Another cause determined persistent costs' increase: it was the rise in wages. The share of direct labour costs (except for some kinds of indirect labour costs such as wage tax contributions to social security, etc.) in total costs of the production sphere increased in 1991 relative to 1990 by 2.3 percentage points (from 14.2 per cent to 16.5 per cent). The increase in labour costs meant that in 1991 the labour force was overpaid (in relative terms). A wage-productivity analysis confirms this conclusion. In industry, the productivity of labour coefficient (percentage increase of monthly wage over increase of nominal labour productivity) amounted to 1.87 in 1991. In construction the situation was slightly better because the increase in nominal labour productivity by 46.7 per cent was associated with 'only' an 86.4 per cent increase in the average wage (1.27 per cent increase in wage for 1 per cent increase in nominal labour productivity).

As I mentioned above, there are other cost elements that are derivatives of wages. As a result, the increase in wages by one zloty gives the rise in total costs by and large by two zlotys. Moreover, many social security payments are set as a fixed percentage of the average wage.

Materials were used wastefully. After some economizing in this respect in 1990 (inventories/output ratio fell during this year from 0.28 to 0.18), the ratio went up to 0.20.[9]

## FISCAL POLICY AND TAX DISCIPLINE

Fiscal developments in the first three quarters of 1990 were surprisingly favourable. The budget was balanced and the budgetary spending kept the public services' sector in a reasonably good financial condition. The first symptoms of budgetary crisis came into sight in the last quarter of 1990. Budget deficit in that quarter amounted to 4.9 trillion zl. which equalled 10 per cent of quarterly expenditure.[10]

Firstly, excellent fiscal results at the beginning of 1990 were partly illusory, and so were the receipts of enterprises which came from devaluation and 'inflationary rent'. The receipts were illusory but the cost push was real. The economy started to pay real money for oil, gas, etc.

This inevitably increased costs in the public service sector and exerted an upward pressure on budget expenditures. Unfortunately, it was these illusory revenues, rather than real cost increases, that were taken into consideration by the government. These resulted in the decision (taken in July 1990) to spend the budgetary surplus.[11] The whole year of 1990 was wasted in the sense that no efforts were taken to rationalize public finances (employment in the budgetary sphere – despite the liquidation of the secret police, reduction in the army and so on – even increased).

Despite these cost increases and – partly unavoidable – fall in output, a budgetary crisis was not inevitable. However, a better result would have required higher tax and spending discipline. Neither of the two occurred.

In tables 4.8 and 4.9, I present data describing the tax discipline (these data concern mostly – but not exclusively – SOEs). They indicate that arrears in taxes exceeded budget deficit in the first half of the year and nearly equalled it in the second. A question might be asked if it were possible for the enterprises in aggregate to pay the taxes due, given the overall zero profits registered in that sector?

*Table 4.8*   Taxes on enterprises in Poland in 1991 (A = taxes due; B = taxes actually paid in trillion zlotys)

|  | A | B | B/A |
|---|---|---|---|
| Turnover tax and wage tax | 77.3 | 71.8 | 0.93 |
| Income tax | 42.5 | 40.0 | 0.94 |
| Assets tax | 22.5 | 17.5 | 0.78 |
| Excess wage tax | 37.0 | 24.0 | 0.65 |
| Total | 179.3 | 153.3 | 0.85 |

*Source:* Informacja Głównego Urzędu Statystycznego; Informacja o sytuacji społeczno-gospodarczej kraju (various issues)

*Table 4.9*   Budget deficit and tax discipline

| Period | Income tax | Turnover tax | Assets tax | Wage tax | Excess wage tax | Total | Budget deficit | Arrears/ Budget deficit ratio |
|--------|-----------|-------------|-----------|----------|-----------------|-------|----------------|------------------------------|
| | | | | *in trillion zl.* | | | | *per cent* |
| I–III | . | . | . | . | . | 6.4 | 6.0 | 107 |
| I–VI | 1.7 | 0.7 | 2.6 | 0.6 | 9.2 | 14.8 | 14.1 | 105 |
| I–IX | 2.1 | 2.1 | 3.8 | 1.6 | 10.5 | 20.2 | 23.6 | 86 |
| I–XI | 2.1 | 2.5 | 4.9 | 2.7 | 12.0 | 23.2 | 27.9 | 83 |
| I–XII | 2.5 | 2.5 | 5.0 | 3.0 | 13.0 | 26.0 | 30.6 | 86 |

*Note:* [a]estimated data
*Source:* see table 4.8

In my opinion it was possible for SOEs to pay the taxes. It was quite probable that many enterprises (at least 39 per cent of them which were in the red) could not pay the so-called 'dividend' (assets tax). But all the remaining tax liabilities arose only when sales receipts were registered, and it was only a management decision to raise wages with the full understanding that there would not be enough money to pay wage-bill taxes (and sometimes other taxes as well).

Two particular habits have developed in SOEs over time. The first is that 'wages must be paid'. The second is that they must be paid at the same level regardless of sales and SOEs' financial situation.

These two habits resulted in a third one. The accepted sequence of payments has been the following: first to pay wages, then bills for delivered goods and services, finally – taxes. As data in table 4.8 show, Balcerowicz's team, regarded by many as liberal in the orthodox sense, did nothing to change these habits. It is another question whether it was possible to do it in the situation where there were eight thousand fully independent SOEs managed by workers' councils.

Another cliché of socialist propaganda (also used by 'Solidarity' in its struggle against the Communist Party) is 'the need to help the poor'. It is pensioners who are singled out as the largest group of 'the poor'. Indeed, it is a large group of eight million (nearly 22 per cent of the entire population) and – in fact – it is a powerful lobby.

However, statistical data do not confirm the fact that they are poor. In 1990 the relation between the average retirement pay and the average wage was 0.53. Given the fact that a smaller number of household members live on one source of income in pensioners' families than in those of the employed, income per capita of the former in 1990 reached 95 per cent of per capita income of the latter (excluding the families of the unemployed). Moreover, given the lower propensity to save in the former, expenditures per capita in this group were 5 per cent higher than in employees' families. Nobody is questioning the fact that many of the Polish elderly are in quite a difficult situation, but things should be seen in proper perspective. Statements about extreme poverty of retirees in Poland are simply not true.[12]

Despite the foregoing, the parliament 'took care' of this group and decided on a huge rise in retirement payments that caused an enormous increase in budgetary subsidies to the social security. An average pension jumped in 1991 by 90 per cent in nominal terms and by 12 per cent in real terms, while budgetary subsidies to the social security system rose from 10 to 33 trillion zl. It was quite possible to avoid the erosion of the budget balance if the government resisted the populist pressure in this respect.

## SOEs ON THE MARKET: AN ATTEMPT AT A CONCLUSION

Macroeconomic outcome depends on the behaviour of enterprises. Seventy years ago Ludwig von Mises wrote: 'It is now generally recognized that there is no internal pressure to reform and improvement of production in socialist undertakings'.[13] After seventy years of experience, we may add that there is no possibility of putting external pressure on SOEs to force them to reform and improve their performance, either.

The system of SOEs functioning in Poland should be recognized as the 'market socialism'. In fact, SOEs, fully controlled by workers (by trade unions and workers' councils), are operating on the free market.

The only difference between SOEs existing in Polish reality and the theoretical 'Illyrian' syndicalistic enterprises described by Benjamin Ward[14] is in the area of wages. It should be remembered that in syndicalist Illyria wages were established and fully controlled by the government and the only way to raise receipts by workers was to increase profits, therefore Poland is today more socialist than Illyria.

There are two consequences of this situation. The first is the paradoxical response of SOEs to changes in economic parameters.[15] The second consequence is a tendency of wage maximization. Assuming that there was in Poland a normal economy with normal profit maximizing enterprises, it would be impossible to raise wages at such a rate as shown above. Also, it would be impossible to disregard the duty to pay taxes. In consequence, it would be impossible to create such a huge budgetary deficit.

The lack of tax discipline in SOEs could be presented as the lack of consistency on the part of the government in its macroeconomic policy. The government should be blamed for resurrecting the situation in which SOEs perform with the soft budget constraint. As I suggested above, the relaxation of fiscal policy was done mostly for political reasons.

At this point, a stronger hypothesis should be formulated. It is quite probable that there is no real possibility in a fully democratic country, in which two thirds of the workforce is employed in the public sector, to impose on SOEs any strong budget constraint. Under these circumstances every economic decision has a strong political character. The frequently described 'politicization of the economy in a Soviet type State' has not vanished; it has even intensified. In this sense, a SOE is not only – as Ludwig von Mises said – 'a dead limb in the economic organism'. Worse than that, it is 'a weed poisoning the market economy'.

## INSTITUTIONAL DEVELOPMENTS

The rapid change in the institutional structure could be the answer to badly performing SOEs. It seems that efforts should have concentrated on three processes:

1   privatization of SOEs
2   changes in the management of still existing SOEs and
3   tightening the environment for SOEs, more specifically looking for strong budget constraint.

*Prima facie*, it seems that there were significant successes in the privatization campaign in 1991. The privatization process began in 1128 SOEs. These enterprises employed about 10 per cent of the total of the state enterprise sector and possessed nearly 14 per cent of the total SOEs' assets.

On the other hand, slowness of privatization procedures should be noted here. Over three hundred SOEs have been included in the traditional privatization programme (i.e. by sale of shares). But by the end of 1991 it was completed in only twenty-six of them. In other words, in

December of 1991, there were 104 SOEs in which privatization procedures had lasted for over one year. It kept SOEs' managers and workforce in suspense throughout the whole period.

The second procedure of privatization, the liquidation of permanently unprofitable SOEs and their sale (as a whole or partially) to private buyers, gave better results. Nearly a thousand (950) SOEs were subject to this procedure. Incomplete data show that, by the end of 1991, 198 of these SOEs were partially sold. By the end of October 1991, 53 of them were sold as going concerns, 24 of them amalgamated into joint stock companies with private shareholders and 354 of them were leased to the workforce (by the end of November 1991). In 200 cases there was no decision yet made. However, 'privatization through liquidation' has obvious weaknesses. First, the lack of domestic capital in Poland results in the fact that only smaller SOEs may be privatized in this manner. Second, there is a moral hazard issue involved, because the worse the financial situation is, the better are the prospects for the workforce to buy the enterprise for a penny. Third, in over a half of the cases, assets were not sold but leased to employees and, to say the least, a higher efficiency of collective leasing was not an established fact.

The question of whether it has been at all possible to speed up privatization and how it could be achieved is still under discussion. However, it may be expected that under any circumstances the privatization of over eight thousand SOEs must take years.[16] Therefore, some restructuring before privatization is necessary as well. The most obvious type of change from the economic point of view and the most difficult from the political standpoint is the liquidation of the so-called 'Bermuda triangle' of management. This label is used to describe the situation in which the managers of SOEs are under strict control of both the trade union and workers' council. The concept of managerial contracts were devised here as an antidote. However, by the end of 1991 there was only one working case of such a contract (in a Warsaw engineering enterprise 'Vis').

The improved environment of SOEs should impose stricter budget constraint on them. Changes in fiscal and credit policies seem to be necessary here. First, tax rates should be established at realistic levels, but these moderate taxes should be collected in a consistent manner. The long debate about the excess wage tax became irrelevant because of the common boycott of this tax by SOEs. In such a situation much stronger wage restraint, as for example wage freeze in non-profitable SOEs, is absolutely necessary.

Changes in money and banking, apart from improving in macroeconomic monetary policy, as suggested in the second section of this chapter, should be based on the privatization of the banking sector. Special symbiotic relationships between SOEs and state banks were created during 45 years of socialism. As a result, a state bank still prefers SOEs to private enterprises. For state banks (owned by 'nobody'), the creditworthiness of their clients is not a serious matter. They are inclined to lend money to large SOEs even when the insolvency of the latter is an open secret. Obviously, in the longer run, such behaviour is suicidal for state banks as well. But they do not think in those terms.

The first symptoms of the banking sector's crisis begin to be visible. In January–September 1991 the profitability rate (profit/cost ratio) in the banking sector dropped from 83 per cent (analogous period of 1990) to 29 per cent. In the nine banks which began privatization procedures in 1991 the share of bad (irrecoverable) credits in their total credits amounted to 25 per cent, which was two-and-a-half times more than a year before. And it must be remembered that privatization started with the best banks!

It was very important that privatization procedures in the banking sector eventually began in 1991. By the end of that year, two state banks were transformed into joint-stock companies, with the dominant shareholding by the state. Nine other banks were transformed into joint-stock companies with 100 per cent state ownership. This is the first stage of privatization. In the second stage, and this seems to be an excellent idea, these banks will have Western commercial banks as minority shareholders (this is the so-called 'twinning' arrangement). Moreover, seven private banks with the participation of foreign capital and 68 domestically-owned private banks began to work. Ergo, some efforts were made in this long neglected field. However, in 1991 over 90 per cent of credit supply was still controlled by state banks.

## IN PLACE OF A CONCLUSION

Economic results of 1991 were ambiguous. Many indicators, such as output or investment, suggested that the crisis continued. On the other hand, many other signals, such as the boom in both formal and informal private sector adjustment and a marked increase in consumption, revealed a totally different picture. The question of which picture is true is an interesting one.

However, in my opinion, it is not the most important issue. It was evident for the majority of believers in the market reform in post-socialist countries that some 'costs' of this transformation would have to be incurred. It should also be quite obvious that some errors would inevitably be made in macroeconomic policy in the course of this transformation. Therefore, it is not the economic outcomes and the macro-policy errors that should be the main criterion of the assessment.

The reform may be described as a race against time. In a short period of time, the new structure of the economy must be created. After this short period, there must be visible effects of the working of the new economic system. Otherwise, social support for the reform will fade out. There are some signs that this moment will come soon.[17] In this context, the institutional development must be regarded as much too slow.

## NOTES

1 'Larger' refers here to non-agricultural enterprises employing over 50 people in industry and construction and over 20 employees in other kinds of economic activity. Such firms gave 72 per cent of total output in 1990. In the present report the word 'enterprise' is used in this sense. The term 'economic units' (or 'firms') has a somewhat wider denotation and includes also housing co-operatives and agricultural farms.
2 According to GUS estimates output of small industrial enterprises increased in 1991 by 15 per cent.
3 The best-known adherent of this idea is S. Kurowski. See, for example, his 'Anatomia stabilizacji (Anatomy of Stabilization)', *Życie Gospodarcze*, 24 November 1991.
4 The exact amount of this 'bad budget debt' remains unknown.
5 Foreign exchange outflows to the former Soviet Union are sometimes estimated at 1 billion US dollars.
6 J. Winiecki, 'The inevitability of a fall in output in the early stages of transition to the market', *Soviet Studies*, vol. 126, no 4, 1991.
7 K. Dziewulski, 'Kogo protegować? [Who should be protected?] *Życie Gospodarcze*, 2 February 1992.
8 J. Winiecki, 'Post-Soviet-type economies in transition: what we learned from the Polish transition programme in its first year' (part IV, 'Behaviour of state owned enterprise'), *Weltwirtschaftliches Archiv*, vol. 126, no. 4, pp. 765–90.
9 Nominal value of inventories at the end of the year/nominal value of output in the year ratio.
10 I must mention again that 2.5 trillion zl. calculated as the budgetary revenue in 1990, was effectively paid in January–May 1991. Including these arrears in payments budgetary deficit in the last quarter amounted to 7.5 trillion zl. i.e. 10 per cent of GDP.

11  The political factor of the approaching presidential election was probably the other cause of this decision.

12  Two additional factors support the foregoing. First, a number of retirees are farmers who get their food supplies directly from their plots of land. Second, many sectoral privileges give the employees the opportunity to retire at the age of 55 to 60. A majority of those continue to work and nearly double their income. Obviously, there are many old people (mainly the infirm and those living alone) who are in real need. However, this is rather a problem for specially targeted social aid (which unfortunately hardly exists in Poland).

13  Ludwig von Mises, 'Die Wirtschaftsrechnung im sozialistischen Gemein-wesen', *Archiv fuer Sozialwissenschaften*, vol. 47, 1920 (quotation from English edn, 'Economic calculation in the socialist commonwealth', in F.A. Hayek (ed.), *Collectivist Economic Planning*, London, 1935, p. 118).

14  B. N. Ward, *The Socialist Economy: A Study of Organizational Alternatives*, New York, 1967 (esp. ch. 8, 'Illyria: Market Syndicalism').

15  However, it remains an open question whether 'the Ward theorems' hold in Polish reality.

16  Especially in the context of very timid participation of foreign capital in the privatization in Poland. Total investment (i.e. buying of shares of privatized SOEs) by foreign capital amounted to about 140 million dollars in 1991. Largest investors were Philips and Thompson, both with investment equal to 35 million dollars. This should be compared with a billion dollars which Poles paid for foreign cars (see n. 5).

17  For example, a survey of public opinion made by the private Institute of Social Research in Sopot in January 1991 indicated that 50 per cent of respondents were against privatization and 60 per cent of them were against importing foreign capital. For a brief summary of the results of this poll see *Gazeta Wyborcza*, 4 February 1992.

# 5 Yugoslav survey

*Zeljko Rohatinski*

## DETERMINANTS OF ECONOMIC ACTIVITY

A sharp recession, accompanied by a rapid deterioration of the balance
of payments, a fall in foreign exchange reserves, and a reacceleration of
inflation brought the Yugoslav economy by mid-1991 to the verge of
material and financial collapse. The underlying causes of this collapse
have the characteristic that under present conditions they cannot be
quickly neutralized to any major extent, not even by one-sided monetary
impulses. The reason for this is that the scale of present disruptions in
the real economic sphere has resulted in the creation of 'black holes' in
the financial sphere, such that they would very quickly absorb any
increase in the money stock without simultaneously improving the
economy's financial situation. Also, it would not substantially increase
the real demand for output – especially in the long run.

The immediate cause of this lies in the continuation of markedly
negative trends carried over from 1990, resulting from the unreadiness
of economic and political organizations of all levels to distribute
functionally the costs of the deflationary macroeconomic policy. Other
contributing factors were the economically irrational attempts to charge
these costs – for the sake of social peace – to other categories than
factor incomes or social entitlements arising from these incomes. This
has undermined the consistency of macroeconomic policy and made its
conduct suboptimal with regard to both their anti-inflationary objec-
tives and the economically tolerable price paid for its realization. This
has, in substance, resulted in complete failure to keep monetary
aggregates and gross labour costs, or rather the funds for financing
personal consumption, within the framework corresponding to preconditions for the establishment of overall, especially external, equilibrium

at the fixed level of the dinar's exchange rate, i.e. without inflation. This has at the same time resulted in a strong appreciation of the exchange rate with destructive consequences for both the balance of payments and domestic production.

Attempts to redefine and create these preconditions by measures of economic policy made at the beginning of 1991 proved equally unsuccessful because the change in the dinar's exchange rate (28.6 per cent devaluation) was not accompanied by the adoption and efficacious implementation of any measures for the efficient macroeconomic regulation of gross labour costs, i.e. wages and salaries and the revenues (expenditures) of the public sector. Thus in a very short time these costs caught up with and exceeded the real level of the dinar's exchange rate, exercising persistent pressure for its further change. At the same time, economic policy, compelled under the circumstances primarily to cope with slowing down the erosion of the balance of payments (which led to a new devaluation of the dinar in April 1991 by 44.4 per cent), had largely lost its often-emphasized anti-inflationary character, since the 'mutilation' of policy implementation (relative to policy concept) caused by itself a further rise in prices. All this made the economic situation worse, not only at that time, but also for the future, especially because the last two devaluations of the dinar were only sufficient to temporarily neutralize the rise in wages and salaries and the revenues of the public sector, and to bring them approximately into (internal) equilibrium, but at the already attained level of external disequilibrium. They were unable to contribute to the achievement of general equilibrium. Thus, it is the external balance that has borne the burden 'caused' by the non-adopted or non-implemented macroeconomic restraint of domestic demand.

The reallocation of money stock and real purchasing power from enterprise sector to public and household sectors drastically reduced the economy's financial potential and growth prospects. Although the foregoing, together with some policy measures (fixed exchange rate of dinar, liberalization of imports, recurrent monetary restrictions), had arrested hyperinflation in 1990 and continued to check its resurgence in 1991, it has also to a great extent destroyed the 'defence mechanism' of the aggregate economy by which it was insulating its long-standing inefficiency from the international environment, and which in essence boiled down to the preservation of the mechanism of sequential deficit financing, inflation, and depreciation of exchange rate.

Thus, at the beginning of 1991, most important were the strategic problems of the economy which, having lost its earlier 'shock absorbers' in the sphere of economic policy and increasingly also in the economic system, were reflected in great imbalances of a real and financial character. These in turn, together with internal political factors and changes in some external economic and political ones, led to a functional blockage of economic flows. Their direct impact on the aggravation of recession, and especially the tendency of a recession to degenerate into a general economic collapse of the Yugoslav economy, was in particular due to the following factors.

First, high production costs, i.e. low labour and capital efficiency, and a rather inadequate structure and quality of domestic supply (relative to prices). Therefore, the enterprise sector was not able, at the time when exchange rate policy no longer neutralized external effects of the additional rise in internal costs and prices, to compete adequately on the domestic market with imports (freed from tariff and non-tariff barriers). Thus, the share of imported consumer goods and equipment in effective final demand increased from 10 per cent in 1989 to 17 per cent in 1990, and even to 25 per cent in the period January–May 1991, a relatively significant part of which was accounted for by imports of competitive products available also from domestic producers. The negative effect of these imports on the sale of domestic goods was only partly compensated for by an increase in exports. As a result, the contraction in this segment of the market in 1990 only amounted to about 5 per cent of the gross domestic product. A part of the increased domestic demand for imported finished products, especially durable consumer goods, was financed by a decrease in overall, especially long-term, household savings. However, a dynamic rise in this demand segment accounted directly, either through substitution of domestic products by imported ones or through changes over time in the structure of consumption, for at least a half of the fall in production (about 10 per cent in 1990 and another 17 per cent in the first half of 1991). Indirect effects were also significant.

Second, apart from direct competition, the contraction of aggregate demand for Yugoslav-made products was to a significant extent the result of the country's political crisis and multiple economic crises in Eastern Europe and the Middle and Near East, which in 1989 absorbed as much as one third of Yugoslavia's merchandise exports. This share decreased in 1990 to 28 per cent, and in the first five months of 1991 to only 17 per cent.

At the same time, a significant part of manufactured exports of more sophisticated products (earlier sold to COMECON countries) could not be in a short time redirected to other markets. This was largely due to their weak competitiveness on other than a defunct COMECON market. The construction industry and all those engaged in building activities abroad found themselves in a similar situation. Here too, owing to recession on the domestic capital goods market, they were not able to find enough work at home. While the import aspect of the fall in demand for domestic products can be considered as a problem of stabilization policy, i.e. of a short-term choice between recession and inflation (although this issue also has significant long-term consequences), the decrease in demand due to the contraction of the East European (ex-COMECON) market and a sharper competition there by manufacturers from developed market economies is a long-term problem of a structural character. The latter can only be remedied by a significant improvement of Yugoslav competitiveness in terms of costs but especially quality (including technological level).

Third, the significance of the foregoing is further enhanced by further factors which directly contribute to the aggravation of the recession. These are political conditions in the country, that directly or indirectly restrain the flows of goods and capital within Yugoslavia. The outcome of this is a further contraction of the domestic market and a still greater demand for imports. Thus, various forms of internal restrictions on inter-republican trade affected to a lesser or greater extent about 25 per cent of the total value of production. The sale of products within Yugoslavia across republican frontiers decreased in 1990 by about 20 per cent, with a further downward trend in 1991. The fall in inter-republican trade has been an almost equally significant determinant of recession as the net increase in imports.

Fourth, possibilities to alleviate financial consequences of recession, or – even more importantly – to prevent recession from turning into a collapse, have been significantly limited by the rigidities and irrationalities created over many years with respect to factors of production. As they strongly constrain business flexibility, it has been very difficult within a short time span to adjust to the rapidly changing market conditions.

Inflexibility of the enterprise sector has its roots first of all in the strongly biased long-term pattern of distribution of the GNP. About 30 per cent of the GNP was accounted for by net wages and salaries and other sources of personal income from employment, about 35 per cent by revenues of the public sector, so that only about 11 per cent was allocated for investment purposes (the rest being accounted for by net interest payments, as well as social services and welfare-fund). Since, however, a part of these already scant investment funds was used to cover losses, or was in some other way channelled into personal and public consumption, total investment was in real terms 44 per cent lower than ten years earlier. Moreover, the low level of development of financial markets substantially restricted the allocation of household savings for economic investments. The consequence of this was a fast depreciation of fixed assets, especially of machinery and equipment. This not only reduced the economy's competitiveness on both foreign and domestic markets but also – together with high actual economic and non-economic risks of foreign capital investments – hindered its fast reorientation in line with the changing characteristics of markets.

Another cause of the inflexibility of business firms is their low labour productivity, or rather underemployment in the enterprise sector. It is estimated that at the beginning of 1991 it amounted to about 30 per cent of total employment. Given the difficult overall social conditions and their economic and political implications, marked employment changes have been well nigh impossible in the short run. As a result, the intra-firm management was only to a small extent adjusted to lower production level, thus burdening enterprises with increasing labour costs.

A final cause lies in the pressing (but only marginally addressed) question of ownership transformation, with an unfavourable impact on entrepreneurial activities.

## DOWNWARD TRENDS IN ECONOMIC ACTIVITY AND FINANCIAL DISTORTIONS

Under the impact of the above determinants, the present downward trend in the physical volume of industrial production began at the end of October 1990, whereafter its seasonally adjusted level kept decreasing until March 1991 at an average monthly rate of 3.4 per cent. Although this trend was arrested in the second quarter of 1991, the absolute level of industrial production was in the first six months of 1991 lower by 17.4 per cent than in the corresponding period of 1990. These aggregate trends were recorded in all sectors of production, but their intensity was primarily the result of a rapid slowdown in manufacturing of machinery and equipment. Decline of the latter had already begun in August 1990 and its output level in the period January–June 1991 amounted only to 75 per cent of the corresponding figure for the same period of 1990. As the output fall was somewhat faster than that of sales of industrial products, output inventories decreased slightly in the first few months of 1991, but their level was only 2 per cent lower than in the same period of 1990. The future dynamics of production – even in the case of an increase in aggregate demand – will to a significant extent be limited by the unsold stocks of finished products.

In parallel with the fall in production and accompanying processes – e.g. bankruptcies – there was a decrease in employment. In the first four months of 1991 it was 8.3 per cent smaller in industry than in the same period of the preceding year. This, however, only partly neutralized the effects of the latent unemployment. As a result, labour productivity declined further by 11.5 per cent. The fall in productivity and the decrease in the rate of capacity utilization by about 20 per cent drastically increased labour and capital costs per unit of production, lowering its efficiency to a level where even possible changes in the external costs elements (interest rates, exchange rate) could not within a short time span contribute in any major way to an increase in this efficiency.

This was all the more the case because under the influence of a rapid increase in wages and salaries at the end of 1990, the fall in labour productivity was at the same time accompanied by a rise in real terms in the level of wages and salaries, whose intensity did not to any major extent alleviate the fall in employment. Thus the level of wages and salaries increased in real terms in the first five months of 1991 over the same period in 1990 by 4.8 per cent (deflated by the retail price index), in spite of the fall in employment of about 7 per cent. This led to a somewhat paradoxical situation. The drop in production resulted in a rise in unemployment, while the pay of those employed significantly increased in real terms despite the fall in labour productivity.

Besides social implications, this made it practically impossible to improve the economic prospects through a relative decrease in net labour costs, which is the usual outcome under macroeconomic and incomes policies in capitalist market economies. The real decrease in monthly wages and salaries in the first five months of 1991 (seasonally adjusted) did not change the situation in this sphere to any major extent. The fall in production in that period was greater than the fall in wages and salaries, which widened disparities even further.

These changes in wages and salaries in the enterprise sector of economy were accompanied by a faster remuneration rise in the traditional public sector (17.5 per cent). Such developments have also a direct or indirect impact on the rise in entitlements in the sphere of public expenditures, where the number of the employed increased by 13.4 per cent! Moreover, since the gross collected revenues for financing the public sector decreased in this period by 12 per cent in real terms, and simultaneously there was a rise in government obligations towards users and providers of services, a budget deficit was one of the consequences.

All this in one way or another led to a further increase in the economy's costs, increasing both the deficit financing and the imbalance between the enterprise sector and the traditional public sector. On the other hand, this extra money growth, despite an increase in relative price of imports caused by the dinar's devaluation continued to a great extent to be used for imports (imports of consumer goods exceeded in the first half of 1991 by 15.3 per cent those in the same period of 1990). Therefore, there was no upswing in demand for domestic products big enough to make the recovery possible. However, such conditions had profound and far reaching negative consequences for the economy, both on the balance of payments and on the domestic financial situation.

Despite a rise in exports to convertible currency countries by 7.6 per cent, aggregate exports fell by 8.1 per cent (due to the steep fall of exports to ex-COMECON countries). This, together with a fall in total imports by 3.7 per cent (imports from convertible currency countries rose by 5.0 per cent), resulted in the first five months of 1991 in a balance-of-trade deficit of 1171 million dollars (390 million dollars more than in the same period of 1990), of which 1001 million dollars was in trade with convertible currency countries. Exports' coverage of imports decreased from 92.3 per cent in 1990 to 88.0 in the first half of 1991.

At the same time, owing to the political crisis in the country and the resultant uncertainty, the inflow of convertible currencies to Yugoslavia fell sharply. Receipts from exports of services decreased by 25.7 per cent, and remittances of Yugoslavs working abroad dropped dramatically by 74.8 per cent, so that the household sector turned from a net investor into a net withdrawer of foreign exchange, with an overall balance-of-payments effect of 703 million dollars deficit, as compared with last year's 601 million dollars surplus (inclusive of the sale of foreign exchange in cash). Thus, in contrast to the first six months of 1990, in which a surplus of 132 million dollars was recorded in current transactions with convertible currency countries, a deficit of 1,535 million dollars was registered in the same period of this year.

On the other hand, a decrease in commercial credits for imports and advance payments for exports (deferred payments, faster collection) were to a great extent caused, *inter alia*, by a fall in the country's external creditworthiness. Coupled with the foregoing, actual exports already partially paid for and the actual payments for previously realized imports, caused the decline in the so-called 'transitional position' payments from 1,136 million dollars in the first six months of 1990 to 651 million dollars in the same period of 1991. With a simultaneous decrease in the use of financial and refinancing credits (due to a failure to conclude arrangements with the International Monetary Fund), the deficit on capital account with convertible currency countries attained a level of 1,566 million dollars. This, together with the deficit on current account, resulted in a drop in foreign exchange reserves to the tune of 2,450 million dollars in the January–June 1991 period. Thus, by mid-1991 reserves fell to 4,660 million dollars only. They were sufficient to finance current account transactions for two months only (or one month, should these reserves also be used for financing repayment of foreign credits coming due before the end of 1991). As regards the enterprise sector's financial situation, according to the data of the annual balance sheet for 1990, it was in global terms characterized by large gross losses. This was due to a relative increase in gross labour costs and the resulting rise in the share of funds for financing private consumption in GDP expenditures. In consequence, losses absorbed 68 per cent of gross profits. The foregoing has had a markedly negative impact on channelling the economy's long-term capital into investment and on the enterprise sector's short-term liquidity position.

The resultant increase in the economy's demand for money and growing problems of financing the public sector exercised a strong pressure on monetary and credit policy in the first few months of 1991. Under such conditions dinar credits of the banking sector exceeded in June 1991 those of December 1990 by 40.4 per cent, while money supply increased by 35.1 per cent, which was considerably more than a half of the amount envisaged for the entire year. To the foregoing we should add the monetary impact of the devaluation working via foreign exchange credits, other net assets and foreign exchange deposits. In consequence, banks' net domestic assets increased in the first six months of 1991 by 64.9 per cent (and total bank deposits by 48.8 per cent). This for the moment increased liquidity, but also made room for accelerating inflation.

Effects began to be felt in June 1991, when prices jumped by 10.3 per cent on a month-to-month basis. Because of the fast increase in deposits relative to the money in circulation, on the one hand, and a relative decrease in deposits of the public sector (owing to current expenditures exceeding revenues), on the other, the enterprise sector's share in the sectoral distribution of money supply increased from 20.6 per cent in December 1990 to 24.6 per cent in May 1991. This was, however, not enough to arrest the general fall in the enterprise sector's liquidity. A sharp increase in the demand for money from manufacturers led to a rise in the average interest rate from about 45 per cent at the end of December last year to about 75 per cent in mid-June this year. Part of the interest rate rise stemmed from the increasing problems of the banking sector itself, as banks' portfolios began to look increasingly shaky due to the fast growth of the share of doubtful or outrightly nonperforming loans.

## LIMITED PROSPECTS FOR AVERTING COLLAPSE

The preceding section shows the depth of the present crisis. It also strongly points to the fact that it is impossible to start coping seriously with the economic crisis without undertaking really radical measures. At the same time, however, the latest drastic aggravation of the political crisis in the country, marked increasingly by elements of a civil war, has substantially reduced possibilities of implementing proper economic solutions before a point of no return is reached. And this critical point is much nearer than it may seem to those who look only at the statistical data, or economic indicators, or at the availability of goods visible through the shop windows. More precisely, this point may be reached primarily as a result of the growing divergence between the diminishing financial and real potential of the economy and the inability of economic policy to neutralize major internal or external disturbances.

The situation will be extremely difficult even if we assume that political compromise will prevent a rapid and definitive disintegration of Yugoslavia and a transition to a 'war economy' under present conditions. The needed radical measures do not stand a high probability of being agreed upon, let alone implemented, not only because of different political options entertained by republics regarding the character of a possible future economic community but also because of differences in their impact on economic, social, and political circumstances in individual republics. Hence, it is practically impossible within a short time to prevent a general economic collapse.

This is now primarily a matter of the economic policies of individual republics, while at the federal state level only the realization of a minimum of common interests can be discussed. In this way, however, solutions of jointly inherited problems become territorially fragmented, and since Yugoslavia (still) constitutes a monetary and customs union, there is a growing temptation of solving one's own problems by shifting the burden onto other republics. Therefore, the basic objective of economic policy should be to prevent such measures at a republican level, which could autonomously induce faster economic collapse.

These are, under present conditions, primarily problems of a drastic decline in foreign exchange and in the extremely inefficient distribution of domestic currency holdings. The former creates real danger that imports may cease altogether and that foreign exchange earned on exports will cease to flow into Yugoslavia. The latter curtail the necessary financial flows within the economy and bring a threat of hyperinflation. What is more, because of the interlinkage between these two problems, the aggravation of one would most likely lead to the aggravation of the other. According to some estimates output could then fall by as much as 50 per cent. In this way the overall level of economic activity would within a few months be reduced to only one third of the real value of production in 1989. Whether this scenario can be avoided only by playing the 'political card' abroad is at the present time really difficult to foresee. But it is quite certain that the risk of playing this card should be minimized to the greatest possible extent. In conceiving and implementing economic policy measures it is necessary to reach a compromise for both federal and republican measures necessary to prevent the economic collapse.

The argument that the collapse is an 'inevitable' price to be paid for the achievement of political aims is not true for all the republics. Thus, some of them would find it easier, due to their lasting or temporary comparative advantages, to endure the consequences of such a collapse. But no matter how close to the truth this argument might be, it is – at the very least – economically a rather short sighted view. For the sacrifices required would be enormous in any case.

The most important for preventing economic collapse is the

preservation of foreign exchange reserves. The ways of short-term alleviation of this problem depend at this moment primarily on determining properly the causes of the present decrease in foreign exchange reserves. In this connection, balance-of-payments data show that 45 per cent of the decrease in foreign exchange reserves was due to the negative balance of remittances and interest on foreign credits, 37 per cent due to the negative balance of foreign credits and financial transactions, and 18 per cent due to the negative balance of visible and invisible trade resulting from a decrease in the coverage of the visible trade deficit by the inflow of foreign exchange from invisibles (from twice in the first six months of 1990 to only 1.1 times in the same period of 1991).

This shows to what extent the fall in foreign exchange reserves was, besides purely economic factors (especially the imbalance among the dinar's exchange rate, the amount of money in circulation and gross labour costs), also the result of the impact of political factors. Thence, there are only very limited possibilities within a short time span to arrest this fall solely by the application of traditional measures of foreign exchange policy – primarily by the devaluation of the dinar.

The need to undertake this measure regardless of its inflationary effect is not questioned but it is simply not possible to get the desired effects – and before the exhaustion of foreign exchange reserves at that. What is needed – but well nigh impossible to implement – is a combination of devaluation with temporary restrictions on the supply of foreign exchange by the National Bank of Yugoslavia for servicing external debt (as well as meeting requirements needed for obtaining foreign financial support). In connection with the latter, and in order to alleviate the other key factor leading to an economic collapse, it is also necessary additionally to reduce the dinar's pressure on the balance of payments, accompanied by a simultaneous reallocation of money holdings from the sphere of consumption to that of production. Under present conditions this can only be achieved by informal co-ordination of activities at different levels of decision-making. Measures of federal institutions should, in this connection, rely to the smallest possible extent on stabilizing the economy by manipulating basic monetary aggregates, while the republics should take appropriate measures to restrict private and public consumption. Whether it is probable – or even possible – to realize such or a similar scenario will soon be seen.

## PROSPECTIVE INSTITUTIONAL DEVELOPMENTS (IF COLLAPSE IS AVERTED)

But if this succeeds – and if political conditions permit – minimum conditions will be created for acceleration of the transformation process of the economy along the lines of a market system, initiated by the systemic changes made in the course of 1990. In this connection the state of the economy will primarily depend on its ability to adjust to the new market conditions and on the speed of this adjustment. On the other hand, the room for manoeuvre for economic policy-makers to tinker with the level of economic activity by means of selective stimulative economic policy measures will be greatly restricted.

It follows from the foregoing that future economic developments should be dominated by the requirements of qualitative improvement of the enterprise sector, i.e. of increasing its efficiency and profitability. What matters less is the level of economic activity of the rate of economic growth. For the quantity changes alone will not solve the problems of quality. The gravity of the problem will be shifted from a macro- to a microeconomic level, where a considerable differentiation will take place among economic agents, both between and within sectors and branches. The evolving market system and the creation of market instruments and mechanisms will enhance the autonomy of economic agents and increase competition among them. The initiation of ownership restructuring will also increase differentiation, but this could be remedied under the new market conditions not, as earlier, in the sphere of production but, almost exclusively, in the sphere of public expenditures (already under restrictive pressures due to the economic situation).

The foregoing tends to indicate that the economy will face a difficult and costly restructuring process, accompanied by a wide-ranging stratification across enterprises. Only some of them will succeed in improving their position, while others will run the risk of falling behind, going bankrupt, or slowly withering away. The emergence of new firms or radical transformation of the existing ones will primarily be based on the profit principle. This will increase the room for significant changes in the sectoral structure of the economy. New lines of production will be started and old lines, whose earlier individual and social profitability was primarily governed by the generally non-market character of the economic system, will often be abandoned.

The speed of this process will no doubt be limited by lack of domestic capital and by uncertain prospects for the inflow of foreign ones. It should be, however, positively influenced by an expected internal release of capital for productive purposes, as the latent unemployment is going to turn into an open one and pressure to invest in one's own businesses will shift the use of savings from consumption toward investment. The intensity of the resistance that may come from the present labour force in the enterprise sector will substantially depend on the quality of social programmes. They should be devised in such a way that the relative increase in social security expenditures should be smaller than the social costs of the preservation of superfluous jobs.

# 6 The transition of post-Soviet-type economies: expected and unexpected developments

*Jan Winiecki*

## INTRODUCTION

Literature on the transition of former Soviet-type economies (post-STEs for short) is growing fast, although given the pace of developments it is still mostly at the stage of articles and mimeo papers, with few serious books on the subject. Debates already begin to shape up: 'shock therapy' versus the gradualist approach, the sequencing of transition measures, choice of privatization methods, etc. They promise to fill pages of economics journals for years to come. The shift from centrally managed (and allegedly centrally planned) economy to the market system became a veritable 'new frontier' for the profession.

What the present writer regards as missing in this avalanche of articles and papers on the subject is an attempt at stock-taking. After all, the Polish transition programme was formulated in autumn 1989, and more than two years have passed since it began to be implemented. The same by and large applies to Hungary. After extensive preparations the Czecho-Slovak programme started in January 1991. Yugoslavia, Bulgaria and Romania, albeit with some reservations (mostly due to unfinished political transition to the post-communist era, see Winiecki, 1991a), also contributed something to the growing pool of evidence.

There exists, then, an accumulated evidence against which various concerns of theorists, including those dominant in implemented stabilization-cum-liberalization programmes, can be assessed. This paper is an attempt at such an early assessment. The present writer looked at theorists' concerns from two different angles: first, whether certain developments expected by theorists did or did not happen and, second, whether certain developments that did happen were expected by theorists. This approach is summarized in tabular form in table 6.1.

*Table 6.1*    Expected and unexpected developments that happened or did not happen in post-STEs' transition

|  | Expected | Unexpected |
|---|---|---|
| Happened |  | a |
| Did not happen |  | X |

*Note:* [a]There is a need for further subdivision of this class of developments: those that were noticed by the profession and those that passed largely unnoticed

The selection of issues that are seen as being of concern to theorists is of necessity personal. Another theorist would, in all probability, make a somewhat different selection (especially in the – of necessity – more arbitrary choice of developments that surprised theorists). But even with all possible arbitrariness the approach yielded interesting insights.

One of the most important is that only a small part of theorists' expectations as to the problems of transition did, in fact, materialize. Transition to the market turned out to be a much more uncharted journey than had been suggested by believers through simple (one is tempted to say, simplistic) recommendations transplanted from economies with different institutions and characteristics.

## WHAT WAS EXPECTED TO HAPPEN AND WHAT ACTUALLY HAPPENED

As signalled already, the list of developments in the transition process that had been expected to happen and did happen is rather short. Moreover, even when certain developments did take place they were more often than not qualified by various 'buts'.

Expectations based on the standard stabilization programme recommended nowadays by IMF (the new orthodoxy called 'heterodox programme'), suggest that hyperinflation is reduced sharply, once restrictive monetary policy is put in place and an attempt is made substantially to reduce budget deficit and particularly its financing through the resort to the printing press. In fact, Jeffrey Sachs, arguably on the basis of Bolivian experience (1987), tended to be even more optimistic, and expected inflation to disappear almost completely (although this was not the case in Bolivia itself, see, e.g., Bernholz, 1988).

This more extreme version did not materialize, but Yugoslav and Polish hyperinflations had in fact ended. But inflation, although reduced substantially, got stuck at levels higher than in known successful cases of stabilization policies (Chile, Bolivia, Israel, Mexico). High monthly inflation rates (e.g., in Poland, apart from outliers, 3–4 per cent per month from April 1990) strongly affect macroeconomic policy, which in turn affects the performance of a respective post-STE in transition.

Considerations underpinning the same standard stabilization programme generate associated expectations of reduction in budget deficit, although historical experience suggests that the process of deficit reduction, let alone elimination, takes place at a markedly slower rate. But the pattern in post-STEs has been the reverse of that registered earlier elsewhere. In country after country initial balancing of the budget after the start to transition was achieved almost overnight with surprising ease. However, after some time, usually in the second year of the transition programme, surplus turned into deficit – and usually a fast growing one. This had happened already in Poland and Hungary in the second year, and deficit is looming in Czecho-Slovakia in 1992. Quite obviously, some factors not taken into account in the underlying theory of stabilization have intervened forcibly in the fiscal area. These issues will be considered at length in the fourth section of this chapter.

The same reverse pattern has been observed also in the case of export expansion as an effect of external liberalization. This has been assumed to take place once exchange controls are lifted, substantial devaluation of (strongly overvalued) national currency is instituted, and distorting non-tariff barriers to trade are eliminated. These measures are expected to reveal true comparative advantages. However, the process of finding export markets under newly revealed comparative advantages takes more time than ordering goods from abroad that were unavailable before liberalization due to – now eliminated – exchange controls. Therefore, import surge is generally expected to precede export surge (e.g. see Krueger, 1980, and her later writings).

This is the logic behind stabilization funds set up under the aegis of

IMF. These funds were to help post-STEs in the early transition period to withstand the pressure on foreign exchange reserves due to increased imports, since exports were supposed to pick up much more slowly. The need for stabilization funds has been stressed from the very beginning of post-STE transition and, surprisingly, as late as 1991 (e.g. see Asselain, 1991 and Portes, 1991).

The present writer regards this concern as surprising, for by 1991 it should have been clear that export surge materializes rather early: a steep growth in exports is registered almost immediately after liberalization. In Czecho-Slovakia, the only case where it did not, the fall in imports exceeded that in exports. Thus, also in the latter case there was no need to draw upon stabilization facility. What threatens export expansion is not, as widely expected, an early import surge with its attendant political pressures to reimpose exchange controls and distortionary non-tariff barriers, but late import surge, following export surge. The threat comes from the inconsistency of fixed (or 'pegged') exchange rate, regarded as an indispensable nominal 'anchor' in the standard stabilization programme, with the steady export expansion based on comparative advantages. This is what, *inter alia*, was observed by Edwards (1992) in the Chilean case.

As fixed exchange rate is used as an anti-inflationary weapon the policy bias favours maintaining it for too long. In the extreme case of Poland it was maintained for 17 months during which prices rose by about 300 per cent. It is quite clear that such a great difference between inflation rates in Poland and in Poland's main trade partners could not be made up by efficiency increasing cost-reducing measures. An increasing overvaluation of the zloty ensued, with the resultant loss of competitiveness.

Effects on trade pattern were dramatic. In the first half of 1990 exports amounted to 119.7 per cent of those in the first half of 1989, while imports were only 54.1 per cent. In 1990 as a whole exports rose to 140.9 per cent of those in 1989, while imports were equal to 106.3 per cent. In the first nine months of 1991 exports were 117.9 per cent, while imports were a whopping 196.5 per cent of the equivalent period of 1990. In Hungary the situation was exactly the same, although overvaluation grew more slowly there (due to lower inflation differentials *vis-à-vis* main trading partners). None the less, while in 1990 exports amounted to 131 per cent of those in 1989 and imports were 112 per cent, respective figures for the first half of 1991 *vis-à-vis* those of 1990 were 127 per cent and 177 per cent. In Yugoslavia import pressures were so strong toward the end of 1990 that the currency had to be sharply devalued and its full convertibility suspended.

The issue involved is not well presented in textbooks on international economics, but the benefits of opening up the economy come in two phases. Phase one is rather short and associated with liberalization of foreign exchange and foreign trade. Domestic producers realize that shifting some of the output to foreign markets will bring higher profits. The result is an increase in exports from the existing capacities and a resultant one-off increase in the value added. This is what happened in post-STEs right after external liberalization.

But it is only the beginning of the benefits in question. As comparative advantages are revealed, some goods become permanently more profitable than others. Over time there is, as a consequence, a shift of production factors from less to more profitable activities. A more profitable export-oriented sector becomes increasingly bigger and contributes more value added. However, in order to become a permanent feature of the newly opened economy, the real exchange rate should remain reasonably stable.

And this is what post-STEs that chose a fixed exchange rate regime have been deprived of. The second phase of reaping the benefits in question did not materialize. Real exchange rate fluctuated strongly as overvaluation superseded undervaluation existing at the start of the transition and production factors did not shift to more profitable uses (for the very simple reason that these uses were rapidly losing their profitability). Partial corrections made on an *ad hoc* basis did not help very much and in themselves undermined the credibility of the desired structural change in favour of the export-oriented sector.

The preceding considerations give the foretaste of the stock-taking attempted in this chapter. As can easily be seen, even those not so numerous developments that duly happened as expected did not follow the pattern observed under earlier stabilizations. The following two sections on expected developments that did not happen and unexpected developments that took most of the profession by surprise reinforce this assessment.

## EXPECTED DEVELOPMENTS THAT DID NOT HAPPEN

One more general comment should be made before the beginning of the overview on unexpected developments, be it those that were expected to happen but did not or those that took most of the profession by surprise. In neither case were surprises always due to the uniqueness of post-STE transition. The underpinnings of alternative interpretations allowing to 'expect the unexpected' were already in place in some writings or could have been deduced from the existing literature. Consequently, their adverse effects on economies in question might have been to some extent avoided or alleviated, had that knowledge been applied in the transition processes.

In fact the same may be said about the expected developments that duly happened – but not according to the established pattern of the past. There has been an extensive critique of the orthodoxy of fixed or pegged exchange rate as a solution in the short run coming from economists of varying theoretical persuasions (see, *inter alia*, McKinnon and Mathieson, 1981, repeated in McKinnon, 1991; Murrell, 1992, with respect to all 'nominal anchors'; Walters, 1991; and Winiecki, 1991c). In fact, one of the founders of the new stabilization orthodoxy also began criticizing of late the use of exchange rates as a means of controlling inflation (Dornbusch, 1990). And consequences of an exchange rate 'anchor' for export performance of a liberalizing economy could easily be deduced from textbooks of international economics.

One of the issues that greatly concerned theorists (and those at the helm of transition programmes) was monetary overhang, forced savings in the hands of the population – a legacy of decades of repressed inflation under the STE regime. Solutions proposed ranged from outright confiscation (so-called 'monetary reform'), consolidation as debt, conversion into financial or real assets or correction through the process of price liberalization.

But in fact only the first and the last were seriously considered by theorists, while in all countries considered here (Poland, Yugoslavia, Hungary and Czecho-Slovakia) correction through price liberalization was chosen – wisely – by respective decision-makers. For although there exists a theoretical equivalence between these two options, outright confiscation is politically untenable in newly evolving democracies, as well as requiring knowledge that does not exist about the size of monetary overhang (see Edwards, 1992).

In any case, monetary overhang turned out to be a non-issue after the start of transition. This assessment applies not only to countries where preceding hyperinflation had already wiped out a large part – if not all – monetary overhang, i.e. Poland and Yugoslavia, but also to the remaining countries in transition. Actually, in the former countries an opposite problem emerged. Since the overhang was wiped out, the restrictiveness of monetary policy did not need to be as strong as it was (Beksiak and Winiecki, 1990). As households tried to rebuild savings to the desired levels even at the cost of reducing further the already reduced consumption, decision-makers were free to pursue somewhat less restrictive macroeconomic policy than the one aimed *inter alia* at eliminating the already nonexistent monetary overhang.

The Damocles' sword of forced savings overshadowed, however, actual developments with a resultant larger nominal decrease in consumption than was desirable for a general turnaround in the supply/ demand relationship under new rules of the economic game (on rationale for macroeconomic restraint at the start of the transition going beyond the elimination of disequilibrium and, more specifically, forced savings, see, *inter alia* Winiecki, 1990a).

Another widely feared development that did not materialize was widespread bankruptcy. Although over time more and more SOEs, as well as Soviet style pseudo co-operatives, were regarded as decreasingly creditworthy, bankruptcies were almost nonexistent. When they happened at all, they usually affected small firms.

The foregoing should not be construed to mean that the performance of non-privately-owned firms was better than expected. The case in fact was the opposite (see the next section). But various factors of an economic and political economy nature slowed down the adjustment process under the market rules.

Two factors were decisive for the near-nonexistent selection through bankruptcy. The first is in my opinion related to another nominal 'anchor' of the standard stabilization programme, i.e. to wage controls. In all programmes in question wage controls became a norm, and wage controls slow down the badly needed adjustment process (Beksiak and Winiecki, 1990; Walters, 1991). Thus, quite apart from the theoretical inconsistency of using more than one nominal variable as an 'anchor' (see Claassen, 1991), nominal wage rate controls have had other adverse consequences.

On the one hand, by restraining efficient as well as inefficient SOEs from increasing employment and wages, they petrified the existing output structure. On the other, by restraining inefficient SOEs from increasing wages they reduced considerably the probability of bankruptcies. Although this has been precisely one of the reasons for their introduction, the 'nanny' role of wage controls undermined the credibility of macroeconomic restraint and new rules of the (market) game.

The second factor is associated with the extended tradition of 'soft' budget constraint of SOEs (see Kornai, 1980 and 1986) that did not completely disappear after the transition. In all countries under consideration, with some exceptions concerning Hungary, large SOEs continued to hold strong political clout due to their sheer size and resultant unemployment consequences. The political economy of 'soft' budget constraint under the transition regime will be discussed, however, in the next section of the paper.

Yet another major threat to stabilization that did not materialize is an import surge that was supposed immediately to follow external liberalization. As stressed earlier, this was generally the rationale behind the establishment of stabilization funds in economies liberalising their foreign economic relations. But import surges preceding export expansion did not happen, and the explanation why this was not necessarily so could be found in the comparative economic systems literature (see Winiecki, 1983, 1985; repeated in Winiecki, 1988, and Ellman, 1989).

STEs were characterized by very strong import pressures because SOEs preferred imports from Western market economies to lower quality domestic products (or those from other COMECON countries). Since they paid the same price for products of differing quality, they always pressed for imports originating from the West. Also, they tried to ensure excessive inventories of imported high quality inputs. It was a part of the system-specific high inventory-to-output ratio policy of state enterprises that could afford to disregard the usual financial constraints.

With the new rules of the game price differentiation introduced an element of choice between domestic and imported goods. If price differential has been larger than quality differential SOEs chose domestic over imported inputs. Also, they started reducing high levels of inventories that became more difficult to finance under new rules reinforced by macroeconomic restraint. A not unexpected result, in the light of the preceding considerations, was a sharp fall in imports exceeding the aggregate fall in domestic output in all countries in question (Czecho-Slovakia being an exception). Stabilization funds were left unused everywhere.

But the early fall in imports instead of the expected surge was only a part of an even more puzzling development that took most of the profession by surprise. The present writer has in mind the unusually deep fall in output. For if prices in post-STE stabilizations behaved on a 'yes-but' basis (they sky-rocketed after liberalization but later stabilized at higher than expected levels), output behaved completely outside expectations. This story, however, belongs properly to another category of unexpected developments.

## UNEXPECTED DEVELOPMENTS THAT SURPRISED DECISION-MAKERS AND THE ECONOMIC PROFESSION

There are serious problems with expectations based on the standard stabilization programme. In the model underlying the 'heterodox' programme (see Dornbusch and Fischer, 1986) policies aiming at elimination of hyperinflations (and severe disequilibria) concentrate on reduction of aggregate demand through restrictive monetary policy and rapid decrease in budget deficits. Severe restraint, i.e. the 'shock treatment', is preferred, as more credible, than gradual restraint. This credibility is reinforced by nominal 'anchors', that by freezing some nominal variables help to drive down inflationary expectations.

A natural – one would say textbook – consequence should be the fall of output. The model says nothing either about the degree of macroeconomic restraint necessary to eliminate hyperinflation or severe disequilibrium nor about the resultant fall in output. This is what one might expect from the programme based on the new orthodoxy with the extent of output fall corresponding, intuitively, to the level of hyperinflation or disequilibrium. It is, then, even more surprising that empirical analysis of earlier applications of such programmes resulted in rather shallow recessions or, as in the case of Israel, even in small expansion (see, *inter alia*, Bruno, 1986 and 1991; Kiguel and Liviatan, 1990; Corbo and Solimano, 1991).

Programmes, the applications of which seem to contradict the underlying theory, should be immediately suspect (and certainly do not deserve the name of orthodoxy, whether old or new!). Be that as it may, almost nobody among the protagonists of the standard stabilization programmes expected the extent of output fall that took place in almost all countries in question plus East Germany. Hungary, which decided in favour of gradualism, performed differently with respect to the initial output fall (although not with respect to the aggregate output fall over the period under consideration).

Initial fall in industrial output in the first year of the transition amounted to over 40 per cent in East Germany and some 25–30 per cent in Poland and Czecho-Slovakia. Only in Yugoslavia was it much lower (over 10 per cent in 1990), as macroeconomic policy became traditionally lax later in the year, when effects of the squeeze began to be felt.

It has been posited by this author on several occasions (Winiecki, 1990a, 1991b and 1991d) that substantial fall of output was to be expected on the basis of the existing knowledge on the behaviour of enterprises in the STE. The very change from a wasteful Soviet economic system entails an autonomous fall in output, quite apart from the degree of restraint of macroeconomic policy or external environment.

The 'mystery of vanishing output' is in fact rather simple. The STE was known for its persistent shortages to which economic agents, especially SOEs enjoying 'soft' budget constraint, adapted by hoarding inputs, fixed assets and labour. The best-known are probably very high inventory-to-output ratios. To give an example, according to Shmelev and Popov (1989), the ratio in the USSR in 1985 stood at 82 per cent, while in the United States it was in the same year 31 per cent.

Quite obviously, once the beginning of the transition brings about the reversal of the traditional supply/demand relationship, SOEs begin to adjust to new conditions of excess supply by drawing down their inventories and simultaneously lowering or altogether cancelling new orders for both inputs and machinery and equipment. Therefrom stems a fall in domestic demand, and consequently output of raw materials, for intermediate products – lathes, instruments, construction and transport equipment, etc.

Not only state enterprises but also households, with their harder budget constraint, adjust to the new relationship. In fact they adjust much faster for that very reason. The re-emergence of goods in the shops is met by purchases of smaller quantities of, for example, food products. Earlier they bought larger quantities whenever they got hold of them, not knowing when they would be able to buy the next batch. Part of these larger quantities were later spoiled.

The foregoing leads to the conclusion that transition from the STE to the market system is bound to entail larger output fall than in other cases of stabilization-cum-liberalization. Of course, not all output fall could be ascribed to the departure from the wasteful Soviet economic system. Therefore it is a legitimate question to ask, whether the size of output fall that these countries registered was necessary to achieve the initial aim of the stabilization programme, i.e. sharp disinflation, or was it excessive? And the question is valid regardless of whether those who pose it understand or accept the implications of the foregoing considerations or not.

A concept of a credit crunch in the state enterprise sector was advanced (Calvo and Coricelli, 1990) to explain why enterprises reduced output due to the lack of resources to purchase necessary inputs. The explanation implies that output was driven in Poland (although it could apply elsewhere as well) below the level of demand. But, Castberg (1991), for example, points out the concept of credit crunch cannot explain the state of generalized excess supply dominant on the Polish market.

The present writer takes an intermediate position between those who maintain, along Calvo–Coricelli lines, that reflation would accelerate recovery and those who say, with the prevailing orthodoxy, that although severe recession was engineered on the demand side (macro-economic restraint), it must be overcome by supply side measures (structural adjustment).

The Calvo–Coricelli explanation applies perhaps to a limited extent, and only in industries that were caught awkwardly in a period of seasonally high credit demand at the start of the transition. Facing initially extremely high interest rates, they reduced output below demand level (with the differential filled by imports). This dilemma is typified by the food industry.

Furthermore, a markedly larger output fall in industries producing consumer goods indicated that other forces were at work besides the inventory drawdown. For it was SOEs rather than households that needed to adjust more under the shift from excess demand to excess supply regime (given their larger inventories due to 'soft' budget constraint). Therefore it was rather a nominal 'anchor', that is, wage controls, that might have affected the level of wages, demand for and, consequently, output of industries producing consumer goods. Thus, some room for relaxation of restrictive macroeconomic policies, including wage controls, did exist there.

This is not intended to be a critique of decision-makers, but rather a support for the thesis that the very limited knowledge of the structure and behaviour of the economy in transition from the centrally-managed STE to a market-type one leaves a lot of room for possible mistakes. Under such circumstances the use of nominal 'anchors' is of limited value, to say the least (on this point see Murrell, 1992).

One of the most important – and strongly adverse – developments has been the impact of an unhealthy nexus of state-owned banks and state-owned industrial enterprises on the performance of economies in transition (Winiecki, 1991c). 'Nobody's' banks that did not care much for the creditworthiness of their clients and riskiness of submitted projects, tended to lend on an inertial basis to those to whom they lent in the past, that is, first of all to the largest SOEs. They were also sensitive to political pressures to support 'important' enterprises. On the other hand 'nobody's' enterprises borrowed almost regardless of the level of interest rates. This applied to a much greater extent to the largest SOEs that were more than other firms accustomed to being bailed out of troubles by communist regimes.

These problems highlighted the neglected role of the financial system that would also entail the search for a solution to the bad debt incurred by SOEs under the old regime. Without cleansing the balances of the banks from bad loans made under central planning, simultaneously with the similar procedure with respect to industrial enterprises, restructuring and privatization turned out to be well nigh impossible. In actual fact, even the expected impact of macroeconomic policy would become doubtful. Few analysts seemed to have been aware, however, of the necessity for early and rapid reform of the financial system (for exceptions, see Brainard, 1990; Marer, 1990; Rybczynski, 1991).

In fact, it transpired over time that monetary policy applied within the framework of the standard stabilization programme in countries with strikingly different property rights' structure generates outcomes that are at odds with textbook-based expectations. Not only did the adverse outcomes of monetary policy come as a surprise, but the spillover effects that affected strongly – and again adversely – the state budget also surprised both practitioners and theorists.

As explained briefly in Winiecki (1992a), a not unreasonable assumption of monetary policy under the standard stabilization programme is that each post-STE enters the transition in a state of greater or smaller disequilibrium, and therefore restrictive monetary policy is called for. An even better reason in post-STEs is to send a signal to economic agents that the era of persistent excess demand has come to an end. A shift to excess supply regime is generated through the monetary squeeze.

What is conspicuously missing in this reasoning, is the typically neoclassical neglect of consequences of monetary squeeze in economies where property rights' structure is drastically different from that in the textbooks. For there is a sea of difference between situations, where SOEs generate 10 per cent, or even 30–40 per cent of GDP and those where they produce anything from 90–100 per cent of the product (as in the case of Czecho-Slovakia at the start of transition, for example).

The consequences were very similar everywhere. Due to the already-stressed unhealthy nexus between 'nobody's' banks and 'nobody's' industrial enterprises, extended monetary squeeze has so far brought largely perverse results. Not only, as stressed already, did output fall somewhat more than necessary, but also its structure got worse. Contrary to textbook expectations that monetary squeeze eliminates the least efficient firms, under the overwhelmingly dominant state ownership the reverse has been true.

Banks continued to lend first of all to their traditional clients, that is larger SOEs, with the consequence that smaller, usually more efficient ones, were crowded out of the credit market. The political clout of the largest state enterprises additionally ensured that they remained least affected by the squeeze. As historically the least efficient largest firms continued to have easiest access to credit from equally dominant state-owned commercial banks, their output losses were relatively lower. And since it has been smaller and better SOEs that faced the toughest credit squeeze, the output of the latter fell often by a larger percentage. Output structure got progressively worse. This is best explained in Winiecki (1991c) and Walters (1991).

The worsening output structure under prolonged monetary restraint generated yet another surprise, namely fiscal crisis in the second year of the transition. This has come about in the most dramatic way in Poland, but budget deficit increased in Hungary in 1991, and this author's assessment is that it may materialize in Czecho-Slovakia as well.

I stressed in the second section of this chapter that the pattern of fiscal developments has been so far the opposite to the one found in earlier cases of stabilization. The budget was balanced relatively easily at the very start of stabilization in each case, while the situation over time got progressively worse.

This surprising result is again rooted in the legacy of the past. SOEs historically maintained large inputs' inventories. Accelerating inflation and aggravating disequilibria in the last years of STE regimes accentuated the tendency (see Shmelev and Popov, 1989, for the USSR and Winiecki, 1990a, for Poland).

Now, the new rules of the game freed prices at which products were sold, while inputs to these products were bought earlier at much lower, controlled prices. Therefore, although output fell and capacity util-ization was low, profitability remained high. As budget revenues depended to a very large degree under the inherited tax on state enterprises' profits, the stream of revenues was sufficient to cover expenditures. This is what happened in Poland, Yugoslavia and Hungary in 1990 and in Czecho-Slovakia in 1991.

But prolonged monetary squeeze with its perverse effects on the enterprise sector undermined SOEs' profitability. On the one hand, profits of better, more efficient SOEs fell sharply. On the other, wasteful giants, living on subsidies and never-to-be-repaid credits, rarely contributed much to state coffers. In fact, the opening up of these economies generated some competitive pressures and resulted in further worsening of their financial performance. Thus, their contributions declined, too. As revenues declined, budget deficits began to increase. The relatively least affected has been Hungary, which began reforming its tax system in the late 1980s. It entered the transition with a more diversified tax system that included personal income tax and VAT. Therefore the fall in SOEs' profitability that also occurred in that country did not affect aggregate budget revenues so strongly.

All countries tried to avoid re-igniting inflation by printing money. Therefore they were adjusting their budgets downward to keep deficits within manageable limits. An unintended but nonetheless surprising consequence of these developments has been a fast decline of budget-to-GDP ratios in all countries concerned (again, except Hungary, where the decline has been much less pronounced for already explained reasons).

There are, however, limits to the decline of budget-funded activities. The resistance increases and shifts the issue from the economic to the political arena, undermining the whole transition process (since in the industrial sector there is a lot of bitterness, not least because better rather than worse SOEs are forced to the wall).

Alongside the emerging urgency of the reform of the financial system, reform of the tax system transpired as another urgent priority. Both came largely as a surprise, since neither stabilization nor liberalization were seen as strongly dependent on financial or tax system reform, at least in the shorter run (on tax system reform see, however, Kaminski, 1989; McKinnon, 1990 and 1991).

## UNEXPECTED AND UNNOTICED

The set of unexpected developments considered in the preceding section has been more extensive than the expected developments, both those that did happen and those that did not. Unexpected developments are, however, even more numerous: for one should take into account the fact that the preceding section listed only those surprising developments that have already received a growing recognition.

On the other hand some developments that the present writer did not consider in the preceding section have, in his opinion, taken place but professional economists seem to continue arguing about them as if nothing had happened. In other words, certain developments were not only unexpected but have also passed so far unnoticed. In terms of table 6.1 they also belong to the upper right-hand quadrant: the class of unexpected developments that happened (whether this was noticed or not).

At least two debates continue with much fervour, although developments in post-STEs so far seem to have already decided their outcomes. The first debate centres on the question whether the return to the capitalist market economy is the only game in town. Market socialism, a long cherished alternative of the left, has been one of the debated choices, while preference for labour-managed firms – a variation on the theme – has had not only intellectual but also political support within some post-STEs and without.

This overview of expected and unexpected developments in the post-STE transition to the market is not a proper place to discuss the merits and disadvantages of alternatives to capitalism (the present writer has done so elsewhere, see Winiecki, 1990b and 1991e). What is worth noting here, is the fact that the gist of the debate in question seems to have already been decided on the basis of post-STEs' 1990–1991 experience.

Contrary to the pronouncements of decision-makers in some post-STEs on shifting back to the capitalist market economy, what we have seen so far in these countries has been by and large market socialism: a world of state-owned enterprises (banks, etc.) affected by the manipulation of market-type policy instruments; interest rates, taxes, exchange rates and the like. Furthermore, most of the unexpected and strongly adverse developments, as well as the absence of some expected beneficial developments in countries in transition, have been precisely due to the fact that state-owned economic agents behave differently from privately-owned ones (see Walters, 1991; Winiecki, 1991c). A version of market socialism with labour-managed firms was also tried in 1990 in Yugoslavia (and to some extent in Poland in 1990–91) and registered similar failures.

Thus, failures of the transition are largely due to the market socialist nature of these economies. It is only with the progressing privatization, both through transformation of the state sector and the expansion of private firms, that this market socialism nature will gradually disappear and, at a certain stage, a capitalist market system will become a reality. Discussing alternatives to capitalism as if these alternatives had not already been tried (and failed!) gives the debate a slightly surrealistic tinge.

The present writer is of the opinion that an even more frequently pursued debate on gradual vs. rapid transition to the market has already been decided by 1990–1 developments. What has been called a 'shock therapy', 'big bang', etc. – and criticized by 'gradualists' – has been a critical mass of stabilizing, liberalizing and other institution-building measures necessary to obtain a degree of coherence among the rules of the game ensuring at least a tolerable level of performance in the transition period.

It transpired, however, that since late 1989 what was thought to be a critical mass in fact fell short of expectations in this respect. Most of the problems these economies encountered stemmed not from the fact that they did too much at one moment, i.e. at the starting point of the transition, but too little. Even on the basis of this chapter's assessment one could add the need immediately to initiate changes in the financial system (cleansing the balances of state banks and state enterprises) and at least short-term modifications in the inherited tax system (reducing the budget's dependence on the state sector's profits).

As stressed by this author elsewhere (Winiecki, 1991f), demand for capitalist market economy institutions is very great from the start, while supply – in spite of strenuous efforts – necessarily lags behind. Improved performance is a result of reducing the gap between demand for and supply of institutions. Graphically it is shown as a decrease of the distance between $S_1$ and D lines in figure 6.1.

Spreading the range of necessary measures over a longer period, as suggested by 'gradualists', has important implications for performance. It means even less coherence among the rules of the game than that offered by the critical mass approach, for the gap between demand for and supply of institutions will be initially larger and the time needed to reduce it substantially longer as well (as shown by the lines D and $S_2$ in figure 6.1). It also means that the improved performance will come later.

In closing this section it is worth noting that part of the gradual vs. rapid transition debate seems to be generated by muddled thinking

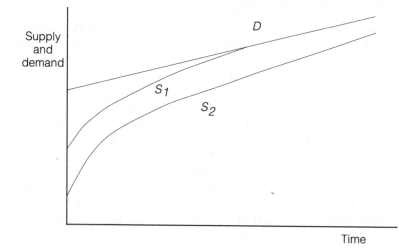

*Figure 6.1*   Demand for and supply of institutions in the transition process

about the problem at hand. Some commentators tend to confuse two different types of decisions taken at the start of the transition programmes in post-STEs. The first type is a decision about a range of liberalizing and other institution-building measures that are to be taken at the start. The second is about a degree of macroeconomic restraint: level of interest rate, extent to which subsidies are to be reduced to narrow budgetary deficit, or extent of exchange rate devaluation. Some commentators criticize mostly the second type of measures.

However, their critique of that type does not make them 'gradualists'. In this author's view, recent experience of post-STEs in transition has already decided the debate in question in favour of a concentrated broad range of stabilizing, liberalizing and other institution-building measures and against a gradual approach taken in the shortest possible time span.

On the other hand, decisions on the degree of macroeconomic restraint at the start of the transition is related to the degree of disequilibrium and the strength of inflationary pressures present in these economies. One may, of course, discuss the appropriateness of chosing one or another degree of restraint or of the length of the time span of restraint, but this, by itself, has little to do with the preference for gradual transition.

## IN PLACE OF CONCLUSIONS

The stock-taking of expected and unexpected developments analysed against the background of theorists' concerns, however imperfect and selective, yields nonetheless an unambiguous picture with respect to the basics of the transition process. A very large, in fact dominant, part of assessed developments came to the economics profession as a surprise of one type or another. Either some expected developments did not take place or, more often, unexpected developments affected – strongly and usually adversely – the post-STE transition.

And, let it be noted, the stock-taking has been selective not only due to this author's judgement of what constitutes important development but also due to the omission of some aspects of the transition. One such, overwhelmingly important, aspect has been privatization. It was consciously omitted from considerations, for it is a very large issue area that deserves a stock-taking of its own (this is, incidentally, attempted in Winiecki, 1992b).

In itself the dominance of surprises over developments expected on the basis of the received theory should not be seen as something extraordinary. The transition from a collectivist-cum-totalitarian regime, with its special economics–politics interface (see Winiecki, 1987, 1991), has been an uncharted path, where no standardized, textbook-based solutions would be expected to apply without thoughtful adaptations.

The fact that they were applied – in the completely different institutional environment of post-STEs – in the form of standardized ('heterodox') IMF stabilization programmes – created certain expectations that simply could not be fulfilled. In consequence, these programmes became as much a part of the problems of transition as that of the solution.

## REFERENCES

Asselain, J., 1991, 'Convertibility and economic transformation', *European Economy*, no. 2 (special edn), pp. 215–41.
Beksiak, J. and Winiecki, J., 1990, 'A comparative analysis of our programme and Polish government programme', in *The Polish Transformation: Programme and Progress*, Centre for Research into Communist Economies, London.
Bernholz, P., 1988, 'Hyperinflation and currency reform in Bolivia: studied from a general perspective', *Journal of Institutional and Theoretical Economics*, vol. 144, pp. 747–71.

Brainard, L., 1990, 'Strategies for economic transformation in Eastern Europe: the role of financial reform', Conference on the Transition to a Market Economy in Central and Eastern Europe', OECD, Paris, November 28–30, mimeo.

Bruno, M., 1986, 'Curing hyperinflation', *Economic Policy*, April, pp. 379–402.

—— 1991, 'From sharp stabilization to growth: on the political economy of Israel's transition', a paper presented to the European Economic Association Conference on Economists as Policy-Makers, Cambridge, September 1.

Calvo, G. A., and Coricelli, F., 1990, 'Stagflationary effects of stabilization programs in reforming socialist countries: supply side vs. demand side factors', IMF, Washington, September.

Claassen, E.M., 1991, 'Sequencing and timing of stabilization policies in the East', International Economic Conference on Building the New Europe, Rome, January 7–9, 1991.

Castberg, C., 1991, *The Polish Stabilization, 1989–1991: Why the recession was created on the demand side, but must be solved on the supply side*, Aarhus University, Institute of Economics (*restore!*).

Corbo, V., and Solimano, A., 1991, *Chile's Experience with Stabilization Revisited*, IBRD Working Paper WPS 579.

Dornbusch, R., 1990, *Priorities of Economic Reform in Eastern Europe and the Soviet Union*, Massachusetts Institute of Technology, December 29.

Dornbusch, R. and Fisher, S., 1986, 'Stopping Hyperinflations: Past and Present', *Weltwirtschaftliches Archiv*, vol. 122, pp. 1–47.

Edwards, S., (1992), 'Stabilization and liberalization policies in Eastern Europe: lessons from Latin America', in *The Emergence of Market Economies in Eastern Europe*, ed. C. Clague and G. Rausser, Basil Blackwell, Oxford.

Ellman, M., 1989, *Socialist Planning*, Cambridge University Press, Cambridge.

Kaminski, B., 1989, 'Reforming the tax system in Poland: general prescriptions of tax design', paper prepared for the Brussels' bureau of 'Solidarity', College Park, Md.

Kiguel, M., and Liviatan, N., 1990, *The Business Cycle Associated with Exchange Rate-based Stabilization*, IBRD Working paper PRE 513.

Kornai, J., 1980, *Economics of Shortage*, North Holland, Amsterdam.

—— 1986, 'Soft Budget Constraint', *Kyklos*, vol. 39, no. 1.

Krueger, A.O., 1980, 'Trade policy as input to development', *American Economic Review*, vol. 70, May, no. 2, pp. 288–92.

Marer, P., 1990, 'Pitfalls in Transferring Market Economy Experience to the European Economies in Transition', paper presented to the conference on the Transition to a Market Economy in Central and Eastern Europe, OECD, Paris, November 28–30.

McKinnon, R. I., 1991, *The Order of Economic Stabilization: Financial Control in the Transition to a Market Economy*, Johns Hopkins University Press, Baltimore.

McKinnon, R. I., and Mathieson, D., 1981, *How to Manage a Repressed Economy*, Princeton Essays in International Finance no. 145.

Murrell, P., (1992), 'Evolution in economics and in the economic reform of the centrally planned economies', in *The Emergence of Market Economies in Eastern Europe*, ed. C. Clague and G. Rausser, Basil Blackwell, Oxford.

Portes, R., 1991, *The Transition to Convertibility for Eastern Europe and the USSR*, Centre for Economic Policy Research, Discussion Paper Series, no. 500, January.

Rybczynski, T. M., 1991, 'The Sequencing of Reform', *Oxford Review of Economic Policy*, vol. 7, no. 4, pp. 1–9.

Sachs, J., 1987, 'The Bolivian Hyperinflation and Stabilization', *American Economic Review*, vol. 77, no. 2, pp. 279–83.

Shmelev, N. and Popov, G., 1989, *The Turning Point: Revitalizing the Soviet Economy*, Doubleday, New York.

Walters, A., 1991, 'Monetary and fiscal policy and aid in the transition', paper presented to the Mont Pelerin Society meeting in Prague, November 3–6.

Winiecki, J., 1983, 'Central Planning and Export Orientation', *Oeconomica Polona*, nos. 3–4.

—— 1985, 'Central planning and export orientation in manufactures (theoretical considerations on the impact of system-specific features on specialization)', *Economic Notes*, no. 2.

—— 1987, *Why Economic Reforms Fail in the Soviet System: A property rights-based approach*, seminar paper no. 374, Institute for International Economic Studies, Stockholm.

—— 1990a, 'Post-Soviet-type economies in transition: what have we learned from the Polish transition programme in its first year?', *Weltwirtschaftliches Archiv*, vol. 126, no. 4, pp. 765–90.

—— 1990b, 'No capitalism minus capitalists', *Financial Times*, June 20.

—— 1991a, *Resistance to Change in the Soviet Economic System*, Routledge, London.

—— 1991b, 'Costs of the transition that are not costs: on the non-welfare reducing output fall', *Rivista di Politica Economica*, vol. 81, no. 6, June, pp. 85–94.

—— 1991c, *The Polish Transition Programme at Mid-1991: Stabilization under Threat*, Kieler Diskussionsbeitraege 174, Institut für Weltwirtschaft, September.

—— 1991d, 'The inevitability of a fall in output in the early stages of transition to the market: theoretical underpinnings', *Soviet Studies*, vol. 43, no. 4, pp. 669–76.

—— 1991e, 'Theoretical underpinnings of the privatization of state-owned enterprises in post-Soviet-type economies', *Communist Economies and Economic Transformation*, vol. 3, no. 4, pp. 397–416.

—— 1992a, 'Monetary Perversity in Post-Soviet Economies', *Wall Street Journal*, February 6.

—— 1992b, *Polish Privatization in Comparative Perspective*, J. C. B. Mohr (Paul Siebeck), Tübingen.

# Statistical appendix

Statistics of Soviet-type economies have been noted for their unreliability due to system-generated distortions and outright falsifications by communist authorities. Direct comparisons of data from communist and post-communist periods therefore entail the danger of often very large deviations from the reality.

Furthermore, the return to the traditional standards of Western societies, inclusive of rebuilding the statistical services and adapting the data gathering procedures to the differing needs of market economies, requires a lot of time. Therefore many of the statistical series presented in the appendix should be regarded as approximations.

*Table A.1*    GDP: annual rate of change in per cent

|  | 1988 | 1989 | 1990 | 1991 |
|---|---|---|---|---|
| Czecho-Slovakia | 2.6 | 1.3 | −0.4 | −16.4 |
| Hungary | −0.1 | −0.2 | −4.0 | −(7–9) |
| Poland | 4.1 | 0.2 | −11.6 | −8.0 |
| Yugoslavia[a] | −1.7 | 0.8 | −7.5 | x |

*Note:* [a]Gross social product approximately 7 per cent lower than GDP

*Table A.2*    Gross industrial production: annual rate of change in per cent

|  | 1988 | 1989 | 1990 | 1991 |
|---|---|---|---|---|
| Czecho-Slovakia | 2.1 | 0.8 | −3.7 | −23.1 |
| Hungary | 0.0 | −3.4 | −9.2 | −13.0[a] |
| Poland | 5.3 | −0.5 | −24.2 | −11.9 |
| Yugoslavia | −0.7 | 0.9–1.0 | 0.3 | −17.7[b] |

*Notes:* [a]in January–September 1991: −18.2 per cent
[b]January–May 1991 over January–May 1990

*Table A.3*   Private consumption: annual rate of change in per cent

|  | 1988 | 1989 | 1990 | 1991 |
|---|---|---|---|---|
| Czecho-Slovakia | 4.9 | 1.8 | −1.3 | . |
| Hungary | −4.0 | 1.9 | −4.5 | . |
| Poland | 3.3 | 0.8 | −13.0 | a |
| Yugoslavia | −1.3 | 1.0 | 2.5 | x |

*Note*: [a]private consumption increased in Poland in 1991 according to preliminary estimates

*Table A.4*   Investment (gross, total): annual rate of change in per cent

|  | 1988 | 1989 | 1990 | 1991 |
|---|---|---|---|---|
| Czecho-Slovakia | 4.1 | 1.6 | 3.0 | . |
| Hungary | −9.1 | 0.5 | −1.7 | . |
| Poland | 5.4 | −2.4 | −8.0 | . |
| Yugoslavia | . | . | . | . |

*Table A.5*   Investment (gross, fixed): annual rate of change in per cent

|  | 1988 | 1989 | 1990 | 1991 |
|---|---|---|---|---|
| Czecho-Slovakia | 0.7 | 2.4 | −12.2 | −28.0[a] |
| Hungary | . | . | . | . |
| Poland | −5.8 | 0.5 | −7.0 | −8.0[a] |
| Yugoslavia | . | . | . | . |

*Note*: [a]estimate, *Zycie Gospodarcze*, no. 10, 1992

*Table A.6*   Investment (gross, fixed): in private sector (excl. agriculture): in billion of national currency and in per cent of total investment

|  | 1988 | 1989 | 1990 | 1991 |
|---|---|---|---|---|
| Czecho-Slovakia[a] billion kcs | 0.8 | 0.8 | . | . |
| per cent | . | . | . | . |
| Hungary billion ft | . | . | . | . |
| per cent | . | . | . | . |
| Poland billion zl. | 20.1 | 57.1 | . | . |
| per cent | 1.0 | 2.8 | . | . |
| Yugoslavia billion din. | . | . | . | . |
| per cent | . | . | . | . |

*Note*: [a]total private sector

*Table A.7* Input inventories: in billion kcs and in per cent of annual change in real terms

|  | 1988 | 1989 | 1990 | 1991 |
|---|---|---|---|---|
| Czecho-Slovakia |  |  |  |  |
| billion kcs | 672 | 702 | . | . |
| per cent | . | . | 8.2 | . |
| Hungary |  |  |  |  |
| billion Ft | . | . | . | . |
| per cent | . | −25.5 | −14.3 | . |
| Poland |  |  |  |  |
| trillion zl. | 5.0 | 17.6 | 118.3 | 173.6 |
| per cent | . | 13.0 | −7.0 | −1.0 |
| Yugoslavia |  |  |  |  |
| billion din | . | . | . | . |
| per cent | . | . | . | . |

*Table A.8* Employment (industrial): per cent change (so-called socialized sector only)

|  | 1988 | 1989 | 1990 | 1991 |
|---|---|---|---|---|
| Czecho-Slovakia | 0.0 | 0.0 | −3.4 | −12.3 |
| Hungary | −2.6 | −1.4 | −5.3 | −15.9[a] |
| Poland | −1.7 | −3.1 | −8.2 | −8.0 |
| Yugoslavia | −0.4 | 0.0 | −3.0 | x |

*Note*: [a]January–October 1991 over January–October 1990

*Table A.9* Employment in private sector (in thousands)

|  | 1988 | 1989 | 1990 | 1991 |
|---|---|---|---|---|
| Czecho-Slovakia | . | . | . | . |
| Hungary | . | . | . | . |
| Poland[a] | 1190 | 1500 | 1916 | 2591 |
| Yugoslavia | . | . | . | . |

*Note*: [a]employed in unincorporated businesses only

*Table A.10* Unemployment (end-of-the-year data; absolute figures in thousands)

|  | 1988 | 1989 | 1990 | 1991 |
|---|---|---|---|---|
| Czecho-Slovakia | 0 | 0 | 77 | 524 |
| Hungary | 0 | 12 | 80 | 406[a] |
| Poland | 0 | 10 | 1126 | 2156 |
| Yugoslavia | 1132 | 1201 | 1308 | 1489[b] |

*Notes*: [a]End-of-September 1991
[b]End-of-May 1991

*Table A.11* Unemployment rate (in per cent; end-of-the-year data)

|  | 1988 | 1989 | 1990 | 1991 |
|---|---|---|---|---|
| Czecho-Slovakia | 0.0 | 0.0 | 1.0 | 6.6 |
| Hungary | 0.0 | 0.3 | 2.5 | 6.1 |
| Poland | 0.0 | 0.1 | 6.1 | 11.4 |
| Yugoslavia | 14.1 | 14.9 | 15.9 | 19.0 |

*Table A.12* Wages and salaries (nominal monthly averages in units of national currency)

|  | 1988 | 1989 | 1990 | 1991 |
|---|---|---|---|---|
| Czecho-Slovakia | 3054 | 3123 | 3380 | 3690 |
| Hungary | 8817 | 10018 | 12500 | 16563 |
| Poland (in thousands) | 53 | 207 | 1030 | 1862 |
| Yugoslavia | 472197[a] | 802 | 4281 | x |

*Notes*: [a]old dinars

*Table A.13* Formation of private firms (in thousands; end-of-the-period)

|  | 1988 | 1989 | 1990 | 1991 |
|---|---|---|---|---|
| Czecho-Slovakia[a] | 56 | 87 | 488 | 1131 |
| Hungary[b] | 1.4 | 4.6 | 20.1 | 45.0 |
| Poland |  |  |  |  |
| incorporated | . | 13.0 | 31.3 | 50.7 |
| unincorporated | . | 813 | 1136 | 1420 |
| Yugoslavia | . | . | 37[c] | x |

*Notes*: [a]number of permits issued. Figures include unincorporated businesses
[b]figures do not include unincorporated businesses
[c]End-of-September 1990

*Table A.14* Consumer price index (annual change)

|  | 1988 | 1989 | 1990 | 1991 |
|---|---|---|---|---|
| Czecho-Slovakia | 0.2 | 1.4 | 10.0 | 57.9 |
| Hungary | 15.5 | 18.8 | 28.9 | 35.2 |
| Poland | 59.0 | 260 | 585 | 70.3 |
| (December-to-December) |  |  | 250 | 60.3 |
| Yugoslavia | 194 | 1256 | 588 | x |
| (December-to-December) |  | 120 | x |  |

*Table A.15*   Quasi-wholesale (industrial) price index

|  | 1988 | 1989 | 1990 | 1991 |
|---|---|---|---|---|
| Czecho-Slovakia | 0.0 | −0.7 | 4.5 | 72.1[a] |
| Hungary | . | . | 20.9 | 34.1[b] |
| Poland | 59.8 | 212.8 | 622.4 | 48.1 |
| (December-to-December) |  |  | 329.7 | 35.7 |

*Notes*: [a]January–September 1991 over January–September 1990
[b]End-of-June 1991

*Table A.16*   Households' money income, gross nominal (in billion units of national currency)

|  | 1988 | 1989 | 1990 | 1991 |
|---|---|---|---|---|
| Czecho-Slovakia | 466.7 | 483.1 | 524.9 | . |
| Hungary (preceding period=100) | . | 116.9 | 129.9 | 123.0 |
| Poland (in trillion zl.) | 18 | 68 | 359 | 631 |
| Yugoslavia | 9.4 | 186 | 1234 | x |

*Table A.17*   Households' domestic currency savings (in billion units of national currency)

|  | 1988 | 1989 | 1990 | 1991 |
|---|---|---|---|---|
| Czecho-Slovakia | 265.6 | 277.7 | 267.0 | 306.3 |
| Hungary | 283.0 | 287.0 | 252.0 | 248.0[a] |
| Poland (in trillion zl.) | 3.8 | 8.6 | 40.6 | 85.1 |
| Yugoslavia | 1.7 | 45.6 | 38.5 | 38.2[b] |

*Notes*: [a]End-of-September 1991
[b]End-of-June 1991

*Table A.18*   Households' total (domestic and foreign) currency savings (in billion units of national currency)

|  | 1988 | 1989 | 1990 | 1991 |
|---|---|---|---|---|
| Czecho-Slovakia | 266.5 | 279.4 | 280.5 | 332.8 |
| Hungary | 304 | 319 | 324 | 348[a] |
| Poland (in trillion zl.) | 58.0 | 46.7 | 89.0 | 150.1 |
| Yugoslavia | 7.2 | 187.4 | 183.8 | 270[a] |

*Note*: [a]End-of-June 1991

*Table A.19*   Money supply: M1 (in billion of units of national currency)

|  | 1988 | 1989 | 1990 | 1991 |
|---|---|---|---|---|
| Czecho-Slovakia | 309.5 | 311.1 | 291.2 | 347.1 |
| Hungary | 302.0 | 355.1 | 449.1 | 442.4[a] |
| Poland (in trillion zl.) | 5.7 | 20.0 | 99.9 | 119.5[b] |
| Yugoslavia | 7.2 | 187.4 | 183.8 | 270.0[a] |

*Notes*: [a]End-of-June 1991
[b]estimate for end-of-July 1991

*Table A.20*   Money supply: M2 (in billion of units of national currency)

|  | 1988 | 1989 | 1990 | 1991 |
|---|---|---|---|---|
| Czecho-Slovakia | 529.4 | 547.8 | 550.7 | 672.2 |
| Hungary | 612.4 | 706.3 | 912.9 | 1010.5[a] |
| Poland | 11.3 | 26.3 | 129.0 | 204.7 |
| Yugoslavia | 3.9 | 88.4 | . | x |

*Note*: [a]End-of-September

*Table A.21*   Central Bank's main lending rate

|  | 1988 | 1989 | 1990 | 1991 |
|---|---|---|---|---|
| Czecho-Slovakia | 5.1 | 5.7 | 6.0 | 10.0[a] |
| Hungary | 13.0 | 17.0 | 28.0 | 29.0[b] |
| Poland | 6.0 | 61.3 | 103.8 | 53.9 |
| Yugoslavia | . | . | . | x |

*Notes*: [a]9.5% in the second half of 1991
[b]January–October 1991

*Table A.22*   Credit expansion for enterprise sector (in billion of units of national currency)

|  | 1988 | 1989 | 1990 | 1991 |
|---|---|---|---|---|
| Czecho-Slovakia | 543.8 | 530.8 | 536.0 | 640.5 |
| Hungary | 681.0 | 815.0 | 984.0 | 1018.0[a] |
| Poland (in trillion zl.) | 10.0 | 28.7 | 114.1 | 184.6 |
| Yugoslavia | 3.9 | 88.4 | . | x |

*Note*: [a]January–October 1991

*Table A.23*  Credit expansion for private non-agricultural sector (in billion of units of national currency)

|                | 1988 | 1989 | 1990 | 1991 |
|----------------|------|------|------|------|
| Czecho-Slovakia | 0 | 0 | 3.4 | 63.0 |
| Hungary | . | 18.5 | 42.7 | 53.6[a] |
| Poland | 64 | 432 | 8854 | . |
| Yugoslavia | . | . | . | x |

*Note*: [a]January–September 1991

*Table A.24*  General government budget receipts (R), expenditures (E) and balance (B) (in billion of units of national currrency)

|                | 1988 | 1989 | 1990 | 1991 |
|----------------|------|------|------|------|
| Czecho-Slovakia |      |      |      |      |
| R | 427.0 | 456.0 | 467.0 | . |
| E | 445.0 | 462.0 | 465.0 | . |
| B | −17.0 | −6.0 | 2.0 | −10.0 |
| Hungary |       |       |       |       |
| R | 706.3 | 836.8 | 1008.5 | . |
| E | 718.3 | 851.2 | 991.4 | . |
| B | −12.0 | −14.3 | 17.1 | −114.2 |
| Poland |       |       |       |       |
| R | 10.1 | 30.1 | 196.2 | 210.9 |
| E | 10.0 | 33.7 | 193.8 | 241.9 |
| B | 0.1 | −3.6 | 2.4 | −31.0 |
| Yugoslavia |      |      |      |      |
| R | 4.7 | 60.8 | 477.4 | x |
| E | 4.6 | 66.6 | . | x |

*Table A.25*  Subsidies (in billion of units of national currency)

|                | 1988 | 1989 | 1990 | 1991 |
|----------------|------|------|------|------|
| Czecho-Slovakia | 96.1 | 122.1 | 105.9 | 68.6 |
| Hungary | 166.4 | 186.9 | 184.3 | 166.7[a] |
| Poland (in trillion zl.) | 4.2 | 11.9 | 32.9 | 22.0 |
| Yugoslavia | 500.4 | 3593.1 | . | x |

*Note*: [a]planned in the budget. Actual disbursements substantially lower (by about one third)

*Table A.26*    Exports (E), imports (I), and trade balance (B) with the West (in million of $)

|  | 1988 | 1989 | 1990 | 1991[a] |
|---|---|---|---|---|
| **Czecho-Slovakia** | | | | |
| E: West's data | 4040 | 4390 | 5020 | . |
| Nat. data | 4580 | 4970 | 5610 | 6779 |
| I: West's data | 4010 | 3970 | 5340 | . |
| Nat. data | 4940 | 4870 | 6050 | 6748 |
| B: West's data | 30 | 420 | −320 | . |
| Nat. data | −360 | 100 | −440 | 51 |
| **Hungary** | | | | |
| E: West's data | 4220 | 4700 | 5860 | . |
| Nat. data | 4310 | 4640 | 5570 | 6506 |
| I: West's data | 4160 | 4870 | 5500 | . |
| Nat. data | 4340 | 4690 | 4750 | 6504 |
| B: West's data | 60 | −170 | 360 | . |
| Nat. data | −30 | −50 | 820 | 2 |
| **Poland** | | | | |
| E: West's data | 5870 | 6340 | 8740 | . |
| Nat. data | 6480 | 6800 | 9200 | 14218 |
| I: West's data | 5210 | 6430 | 7100 | . |
| Nat. data | 5900 | 6410 | 5860 | 14247 |
| B: West's data | 660 | −90 | 1640 | . |
| Nat. data | 580 | 390 | 3340 | −29 |
| **Yugoslavia** | | | | |
| E | 9624 | 10519 | 11834 | x |
| I | 10202 | 11971 | 16504 | x |
| B | −578 | −1452 | −4670 | x |

*Note*: [a]trade in convertible currencies

*Table A.27*    Current account balance in convertible currencies (in million of $)

|  | 1988 | 1989 | 1990 | 1991 |
|---|---|---|---|---|
| Czecho-Slovakia | 91 | 443 | −1104 | −(200–400)[a] |
| Hungary | −807 | −1437 | 127 | 490[b] |
| Poland | −563[c] | −1843 | 1093 | −1749[b] |
| Yugoslavia | 2210 | 2010 | −858 | −580[d] |

*Notes*: [a]January–September 1991
     [b]January–November 1991
     [c]including the balance of clearing transactions
     [d]January–June 1991

*Table A.28*   Exchange rates *vis-à-vis* $ (annual averages in units of national currency)

|  | 1988 | 1989 | 1990 | 1991 |
|---|---|---|---|---|
| Czecho-Slovakia |  |  |  |  |
| Official | 14.36 | 15.05 | 17.39 | 29.48 |
| Unofficial | 33.44 | 42.39 | (39.0–40.0) | 32.28 |
| Hungary |  |  |  |  |
| Official | 50 | 59 | 63 | 74[a] |
| Unofficial | . | . | . | . |
| Poland |  |  |  |  |
| Official | 431 | 1446 | 9500 | 10559 |
| Unofficial | 1979 | 5565 | 9570[b] | 10731[b] |

*Notes*: [a]average of the January–October 1991 period
[b]official averaged rate at private exchanges

# Index